ENCYCLOPEDIA
CORRUPTION
IN THE WORLD

Book 4: Perspective of International Law on Corruption

JUDIVAN J. VIEIRA

authorHOUSE®

AuthorHouse™
1663 Liberty Drive
Bloomington, IN 47403
www.authorhouse.com
Phone: 1 (800) 839-8640

Published by AuthorHouse 11/15/2018

ISBN: 978-1-5462-5511-6 (sc)
ISBN: 978-1-5462-5509-3 (hc)
ISBN: 978-1-5462-5510-9 (e)

Library of Congress Control Number: 2018909723

Print information available on the last page.

Thanks to:

My mother (in memoriam), who told me when I was still the assistant of a bricklayer that studying would make a difference in my life.

Eliane Caetano, an advisor and head of my personal office for efficiency and help in the research phase and bibliographic organization, during the five years that made this work a scientific reality and an innovative proposal.

Neither the corrupt nor the virtuous has power over their moral behavior, but they had, rather, power to become one thing or another; so also someone who throws a stone has power over it before hurling it, but does not have it after having thrown it.

Aristotle

CONTENTS

INTRODUCTION

It is common to the citizen who has no contact with the discipline of law to imagine that all national legislation is unprecedented production of his country.

Indeed, a significant part of the legal scholars and professionals working in the area are unaware that since the 1950s, international law has inspired most national legal systems in matters such as bids and contracts, human rights, pimping, drug trafficking, trafficking in arms, organ trafficking and combating corruption against the general public administrations, as we will see in this Book IV.

The United Nations Organization(UN) identifies corruption with public funds as a threat to the democratic regime, since it prevents the state from playing its role of provider of the common good.

We will continue to demonstrate that there is legislation to combat corruption within each member country of Mercosur.

However, this legislation is conceived from an internal perspective, ignoring the current moment of evolution in which crimes and acts of administrative improbity have become transnational.

In this work we identify the corruption as the main obstacle to the implementation of substantive democracy and we advocate for an effective fight by unifying the criminal law because it takes care of the criminalization of the offense, of the criminal process because it establishes the rules of the prosecution of the offender and of administrative-disciplinary process because it represses the deviations of functional conduct that act as fuel for the embezzlement of public goods, money and revenues and, consequently, contributes to the inefficiency and inefficacy of public policies.

In this Book IV, you will learn the perspective of international law on corruption, through corruption indexes in Mercosur; will understand why the international fight against corruption has become necessary;

will understand the importance of international conventions to combat corruption and will also learn about a comparative study on Italian administrative justice and Brazilian administrative justice that we have done since a course on "Comparative Law and Civilistic Tradition", held at the University of Rome Tor Vergata in July 2013.

BOOK IV

Perspective of International Law on Corruption

The Comparative Study of Law shows that national legal systems are heavily influenced by international law.

The student or any professional who works with law, that gives no attention to the comparative study of different systems of law, will be surprised to realize that, in this globalized world many legal institutes of the national order derive directly from International Conventions and Treaties.

Examples include white-collar crimes (also known as corporate crimes), rules on bids and contracts, human rights and anti-corruption rules.

The international community has been slow to do so, but has realized that corruption produces damaging results to modern rule of law, public administration and society as a whole.

This is why the two main international conventions, the Inter-American Convention against Corruption(IACAC) and the United Nations Convention against Corruption(UNCAC), reflect the following concerns and certainties about the harmful effects of this social malady:

1 - That corruption poses a threat to the stability and security of societies by weakening the institutions and values of democracy, ethics and justice and by undermining sustainable development and the rule of law;

2 - That the links between corruption and other forms of crime, in particular organized crime and economic corruption, including money laundering, undermine the foundations for good coexistence and development;

3 - That cases of corruption penetrate different sectors of society and may jeopardize a significant proportion of States resources;

4 - That corruption has ceased to be a local problem in order to become a transnational phenomenon affecting all societies and economies, international cooperation is needed to prevent and fight against it;

5 - That a comprehensive and multidisciplinary approach is required to prevent and effectively combat corruption;

6 - That the availability of technical assistance can play an important role in enabling states to be better able to prevent and effectively combat corruption, inter alia by strengthening their capacities and creating credible institutions;

7 - That illicit personal enrichment can be particularly harmful to democratic institutions, national economies and the rule of law;

8 - That corruption undermines the legitimacy of public institutions and attacks society, the moral order and justice, as well as against the integral development of peoples;

9 - That representative democracy, which is an indispensable condition for the stability, peace and development of the region, requires by its very nature the fight against all forms of corruption in the exercise of public functions and acts of corruption specifically linked to its exercise;

10 - That the fight against corruption strengthens democratic institutions and avoids distortions in the economy, vices in public management and deterioration of social morality

Note that the international community, deeply concerned about ever closer links between corruption and revenues from illicit trafficking in drugs that threaten and corrode society, acknowledged that corruption is sometimes one of the tools used by organized crime to fulfill its aims and, in some cases, interlationally.

An empire as well structured as the empire of corruption requires States to act in a coordinated way to combat it effectively.

The concern with corruption was decisive for the conviction of the international community about the following subjects:

– The importance of generating an awareness among the people of the countries of the region of the existence and seriousness of this problem and of the need to strengthen the participation of civil society in preventing and combating corruption;

– The need to adopt, as soon as possible, international instruments to promote and facilitate international cooperation to combat corruption and, in particular, to take appropriate measures against persons committing acts of corruption in the exercise of their public functions or specifically related to this exercise, as well as regarding the assets that are the result of these acts.

Concern about the harmful effects of corruption has led to the conviction that prevention and reduction to tolerable limits is the responsibility of all States Parties of the Conventions and that they shall cooperate with each other, joining forces with the private and third sector to avvoid ruin of the democratic rule of law.

It was International Law that found the best formulas for combating corruption, through the IACAC and UNCAC conventions, which became an inspiration for national rights and of which we emphasize the following principles that should govern the Nations:

1 - Proper management of public affairs and goods;

2 - Equity;

3 - Responsibility;

4 - Equality before the law; and

5 - Due process in criminal, civil and administrative proceedings.

Know the enemy, draw the strategies and start the fight. This seems to be the path taken by the international community when it decides to make efforts to prevent, detect, punish and eradicate corruption in the exercise of public functions and acts of corruption specifically linked to its exercise.

The task is to prevent, detect and deter more effectively international transfers of illicitly acquired assets and to strengthen international cooperation for the recovery of these assets in close cooperation with national legal systems, fostering a culture of rejection of corruption.

Throughout this work, we try to show how naive it is to want to eradicate corruption. However, we believe we can fully reduce it to tolerable levels.

For this, the best way is to overcome impunity, since it is the main fuel of corruption, which devastates the State's capacity to promote social welfare.

The less tolerance with the corrupt, the greater the possibility of building a wall of fire around ethics and morals in public affairs. If we do that, then we can reach the stage of substantial democracy that our Constitutions so much dream.

CHAPTER 1

Perception Indexes of Corruption in Mercosur

Julio E.S. Virgollini writing on the symmetry of European and Latin American corruption processes says:

> "In words that deal with the Italian reality, but that can very clearly be referred to Argentina or to many other countries, especially in the Latin American area, where extended and prolonged processes of corruption and crime are deployed, FERRAJOLI describes the situation in this way:

> "In fact, in view of the dimensions reached by corruption and the collusion of political power with the Mafia, the Camorra and with the other invisible powers (Masonic lodges, Gladio, P2 and deviant secret services), our State is really a double State, behind whose legal and representative façade had grown a clandestine infra-State, endowed with its own codes and attributes, organized in hidden centers of power, destined for the private appropriation of public property and secretly covered with recurrent subversive temptations. Thus, a double hidden and parallel State that contradicted all the principles of political democracy and the Rule of Law, from the principle of legality to that of publicity, visibility, controllability and responsibility of the public powers ".

The same author (2004: 254-256), making an analysis of the functionality, damages and victimization produced by corruption, says:

"In times of transition, it has been said, corruption favors the processes of economic and institutional development because it represents the opening of integration channels for those groups that, otherwise, by expressing their own demands would resort to violence; in this way, corruption can be functional to the maintenance of political order. In a vaguely similar way, corruption has frequently been linked to situations of economic backwardness or institutional disorder, whose overcoming should naturally entail a reduction in social tolerance regarding this phenomenon; in this perspective, the costs of corruption could be lower than the benefits it produces, because it provides the only instrument available to overcome the obstacles that impede economic development.

That the problem of corruption can be put in terms of functionality or dysfunction comes, at least in part, from the apparent absence of the victim, as the protagonists of corrupt practices are consensual actors: they buy and sell, they exchange benefits voluntarily. In the context of these relationships, the victim is invisible, because in reality the damage occurs in another area and in another time than in those in which the exchange occurs, and also in relation to other people. These types of circumstances are remarkably similar to those that occur in the area of white collar crime, especially when attention is drawn to the frequency with which the victims of these events do not become aware of the damage they have suffered.

5. The damages of corruption

"One of them is constituted by what RUGGIERO calls the metrification of rights, that is, the conversion to private goods, which can be negotiated in the market, of (...) The rights to work, to housing, to health, to education, to the expression of ideas, etc., belong to the sphere of citizenship, but corruption transforms them into negotiable goods, which distorts social justice, whose characteristics should be predictability and equality, to turn it into the result of a private negotiation or an arbitrary or funny concession. (...)

The corrupt exchange is by nature opaque, obscure, it is constituted in the negation of the visibility, what comes from the necessity, inherent to the systems of the representative democracy, to resort to mediators that cover the function of linking with the government the necessities and the interests of citizens. But these politicians have financing costs that must be covered in some way, which is the first incentive for corruption (...)

In addition, what is obscured is the ability of the citizen to verify the fulfillment of the mandate given to his representatives or the content of the decisions taken by them during their function, since in reality they become dependent on the hidden forces. that act within the political parties: political representation unfolds in the most absolute darkness, leading to the moral and political disqualification of the citizen.

This form of victimization is not the only one. According to RUG-GIERO, an additional problem is the spread of corrupt practices at all levels of society, partly encouraged by general impunity, and partly by the growing and more widespread social habit of obtaining some benefit of small and daily corrupt exchanges. The accustomed to corruption that occurs at lower levels reduces the sensitivity to this type of episodes, which in fact end up parity the small individual corruption with the large negotiated. (...) To paraphrase SYKES and MATZA, one of whose neutralization techniques used to "condemn those who condemn", RUGGIERO suggests that the technique appropriate to corruption is, instead, "to forgive those who forgive".

Manuel Villoria Mendieta (2000: 97) drawing a parallel between the states in which the population relies on the government and those in which corruption establishes itself generating distrust, cites Paraguay as one of the most corrupt in the world in 1998. It says:

"On the contrary, they are countries with great development of participatory culture and trust in the State where less corruption occurs -for example, in the Nordic European countries-. According to the "corruption perception index", developed by Transparency

3

International, for 1998, the five least corrupt countries in the world are in this order: Denmark, Finland, Sweden, New Zealand and Iceland. And the ten most corrupt, also by order: Cameroon, Paraguay, Honduras, Nigeria, Indonesia, Colombia, Venezuela, Ecuador, Russia and Bolivia. However, each country has its peculiarities and trying to define common rules is quite difficult. In any case, corruption is the extreme form of the absence of ethics and, due to its seriousness, generates a crisis of legitimacy in the State that demands immediate responses at the highest institutional level before its expansion destroys the system of coexistence (López Caldera, 1997)."

Jorge Luiz Raimondi (2005: 273) in dealing with the illicit enrichment of public officials in Argentina says:

"Unfortunately, the existence of public officials that ostensibly increase their personal assets during the exercise of the position seems to be a constant in Argentine history. At least, this follows from the mere compulsa of the annals of local legislation, in which, throughout the different epochs, the regulations related to the subject are repeated. Thus, for example, on December 5, 1622, King Philip TV dictated Law VII, which established: "(...) governors, corregidores, and alcaldes mayores are not admitted to the use and exercise of their offices, if do not present the inventory of all their goods, and having them, and those who are in the Indies do and present to the royal hearings of the district (...) ", supplementing with the law LXVIII as soon as he urged not to admit in the hearings of the continent to any minister, even before the presentation of the appointment signed by the king himself, if it was not accompanied by the testimony of having presented in the Council of the Indies the inventory of his property, and the law IX - of the Compilation de Indias- which provided for the creation of bonds to answer for subsequent residency trials."

In the context of Mercosur, the variation in the perception of corruption between the years 2000 and 2017 indicates little improvement for better only in the part of Uruguay, as evidenced by the data of Transparency International, which, in particular, does not investigate isolated cases of corruption, but offers considerable subsidies in the scope of researches about world corruption. Here are some data that deserve consideration:

Indexes on perception of corruption in Mercosur between 2000 and 2018
(Among 90 countries in 2000 and 180 Countries in 2017)

Country	Year 2000	Year 2017
Argentina	52	85
Brazil	49	96
Paraguay	No data	135
Uruguay	No data	23
Venezuela	71	169

The Corruption Perceptions Index released by Transparency Internacional (TI) from 2012 to 2017 shows that Argentina and Paraguay the perception of corruption decreased a little, in Uruguay the perception of corruption increased a little, while in Brazil and Venezuela the perception of corruption increased considerably.

Venezuela, recently admitted as a member of Mercosul, is shamefully adding itself to the most corrupt countries in the world. Here is the ranking of 2012 and 2017:

Rank of Transparency International from 2012 to 2017

Country	Year 2012	Year 2017
Argentina	102	85
Brazil	69	96
Paraguay	150	135
Uruguay	20	23
Venezuela	165	169

Juan Bautista Cincunegui and Juan de Dios Cincunegui addressing corruption and the factors of power affirm:

> *"Administrative corruption is not a recent phenomenon but we all have the intuition that it has become widespread in recent years in an alarming manner. The problem is not limited only to the enrichment of some officials and the consequent damage suffered by the State. Corruption has much more devastating effects. It affects the legitimacy of political institutions, undermines morality*

and justice, generates pernicious consequences in economic matters and deepens the crisis of values due to the absence of models of personal virtue and honesty in those who occupy public positions of responsibility. At the same time, it generates blankets of suspicion on honest officials, which de-incentivates probas people to accede to public positions."

Jorge Luis Rimondi (2005: 31-32), addressing the need for transparency in procedures to combat corruption in Argentina, says:

"... It is true that the sentence to the official responsible for an act of corruption in the management of public affairs is based on the strictest justice, but it is no less true that for a State it is more profitable to establish procedures that prevent the acts of this type. It is known that the best medicine is preventive; In the same way, it is more beneficial for the social body to establish mechanisms to prevent conflicts within them than to solve them".

As for Brazil, we have already said elsewhere that corruption has an estimated annual cost of US $ 3.5 billion, according to the Getulio Vargas Foundation, more than 30 billion, according to the Federation of Industries of the State of São Paulo (study conducted in 2010) and more than 100 billion, according to a study released by the UNDP.

It should be noted that the difference between the disclosed values is extremely large. In my feeling they are beyond what the UN divulges.

The question that matters is: How much could the provision of public services be improved if the sums of diverted public money were invested in social welfare?

CHAPTER 2

Why The International Combat of Corruption Has Been Necessary

David Baigun and Nicolás Garcia (2006: 161) say that the economicization of society, the increase in trade and communications, and widespread globalization have increased the scope of corruption and the need to combat it:

> "One can ask why corruption now emerges as an international priority. A first argument is that the phenomenon has been aggravated by the economization of society: the rapid increase in trade and international communications. Another possibility is that certain reforms are spreading from one side of the world to the other creating new opportunities for corruption by modifying the traditional rules of the game, and in some cases, as in the case of Eastern European countries, political change is not always are accompanied by a similar development of the institutions and the incentives of the public sector."

2.1 - Combating corruption in the European Union

Baigun and Rivas (2006: 162-163, 171-172) assert that the fight against corruption must have public policy status:

"V. The anti-corruption policy of the European Union

We have already indicated in previous pages that at first the interest for the repression of corruption is due to the purpose of punishing those actions that violate the community law or harm the financial interests of the Community. The punishment of officials responsible for the collection, management, disbursement or control of Community funds provided they have incurred passive bribery, the abusive exercise of the office, the misappropriation of funds from the Community budget, disclosure of official secrets as well as money-laundering and reception are shown as instruments of a preventive nature in the face of behaviors that harm or jeopardize the financial interests of the European Economic Community.

(...)

We have first of all the Convention on the protection of the financial interests of the European Communities of 29 September 1995, which establishes important principles for the criminal prosecution of fraud in an efficient and homogeneous way in all the Member States."

From the political forum entitled "The World Fight Against Corruption" (1996: 76-81) by the University of Social Museum of Argentina, March 1996, a precious account of the world fight against corruption is extracted. Here is an excerpt:

"The global fight against corruption

Paris - Call it return, commission, pot de vin or simply bribe: the payments of businessmen to officials add billions of dollars per year to the cost of doing business around the world.

Bribes inflate the price of contracts, discourage investment, and have increased the debt of poor countries by a third.

All countries proscribe the corruption of their own officials, but only the United States and Sweden prohibit their national companies from corrupting foreign officials. In many countries, business bribes to get overseas markets are tax deductible. (...)

Corruption has taken a particularly heavy toll on Africa, and many of its business leaders worry that the continent's bad reputation will exclude them from the benefits of world trade. Last August, South African President Nelson Mandela called for international action to "make corruption a more dangerous and less profitable issue."

A recent Swiss study found 20 billion dollars in accounts in the name of current and past governors of Africa only in Swiss banks.

The European Bank for Reconstruction and Development, based in London, which encourages investment in the former communist bloc, called bribes in Eastern Europe a "major deterrent" to foreign investment. And experts say that corruption in China and other developing countries such as Indonesia, Pakistan, Venezuela, Brazil, Argentina, India and the Philippines is widespread. (...)

International bankers and aid organizations worry that corruption undermines the development of the world's poorest nations. "Investors and agents need to have a clean environment if we are to achieve the benefits of global trade and investment," says Kim Jaycox, vice president of the World Bank in charge of Africa.

In Asia, national campaigns to limit corruption also gain ground. In South Korea, two former presidents and several business magnates face charges of corruption linked to bribes that would have amounted to 1 billion dollars. The two-year campaign against corruption in China led to the execution of some low-ranking municipal officials and last year displaced the Communist Party secretary in Beijing. And in 1993 popular distaste for corruption scandals helped end 38 years of the Liberal Democratic Party's government in Japan.

The crusade of the judges

In Europe, a handful of judges began investigating corruption cases that came to power. Italy's clean mamis campaign set the course for a new group of independent magistrates in France, Spain, Portugal, Belgium and Greece. Thousands of Italian politicians and businessmen were questioned and more than 700 were tried for bribery since Milan's magistrates launched their investigations in 1992.

On October 20, 1995, the Secretary General of NATO, Willy Claes, resigned when the Parliament decided by voting to lift the immunity that protected him from the investigations. The resolution was due to accusations that, as an official of the Flemish Socialist Party, he had known illegal payments of 1.6 million dollars from an Italian defense company to the party's coffers to influence the contract for the purchase of helicopters.

In France, more than 100 business leaders and politicians investigated for illegal practices. In 1993, for the first time, a French prime minister promised that the government will not block such investigations. Last year, judicial investigations led to the resignation of government ministers and the arrest of a third party.

"Culture in France is slowly changing," says Thierry Jean Pierre, one of the original investigating magistrates and now a member of the European Parliament. "Ten years ago the bribery and corruption investigation was totally taboo here."

Pierre attributes to the example of the Italian magistrates that he inspired the French judges to pursue sensitive investigations in political terms that had previously been silently abandoned. The judges were also outraged by the 1990 law that granted amnesty for crimes linked to the legal financing of political parties.

(...)

However, the task of exhorting governments to go from limiting the corruption of their own officials to monitoring the activities of their multinationals abroad has crashed into a concrete wall.

For industrialized countries, overseas contracts are a matter of national security, and bribes are a legitimate way of obtaining them. A recent US intelligence work that analyzed illegal payments in 100 major contracts in 1994, concluded that foreign companies that offered bribes won in 80% of the cases.

Provided with this information, the United States has pressured international organizations to match the playing field in the competition for international contracts. Washington wants its rivals to compete with the same rules applied to American executives by the External Corruption Practices Act of 1977.

Global action

At the request of the United States, the Organization for Economic Cooperation and Development has been studying new guidelines for corruption since 1989. In 1994, the OECD approved the non-binding recommendation to urge member states (the 20 richest on the planet) to criminalize the corruption of a foreign public official. Since then, civil groups study the legislation of member countries with an eye on harmonizing national laws on corruption.

After the revelations of fraud in the annual budget of 100,000 million dollars, the European Union proposed to make bribery and waste of EU funds a crime under national laws. The Council of Europe assigned a group to develop an international anti-corruption strategy, which is presumed to present its recommendations this autumn.

(...)

"The 1977 law applies to all North American subsidiaries as well as US-based companies. If those subsidiaries lose a contract due to a bribe, they will want to reveal it, "he explains. "Many French companies are also investing massively in the United States and have to abide by American standards. The French managers want to have a world policy, without exceptions."

In many countries the fight against corruption is becoming a good business. Firms such as the New Yorker Kroll Asociados offer business research and audit services to detect immoral conduct by, within or against the organization. And in France, the accounting firms that specialize in finance and municipal corruption proliferate: there, the intent is to defend themselves against accusations of corruption with preventive audits at the beginning of their mandates."

2.2 - Global anti-corruption Conventions and Norms

The globalization of corruption requires globalization of means of combat.

In this endeavor, if the Executive, Legislative and Judicial branches, and other bodies of Justice do not unite, they will lose the war and the opportunity to achieve distributive justice, which is the basis of the democratic rule of law.

Baigun and Rivas say that one of the useful tools to combat corruption is the harmonization of international criminal law. Here is an excerpt from the authors thinking:

"III. Community legal instruments that require harmonization of criminal legislation on corruption

The truth is that in the call ambiguously fight against corruption, there is no convincing and univocal explanation to the phenomenon, so we prefer to stick in our exposure to summarize the different versions that have given some of the institutional frameworks involved in this fight. However, there are many international legal instruments that have been created and that are currently in the process of being ratified in European parliaments and in other geographical areas or that are even part of the legal systems of some countries; here are indicated only some of the most important among the 21 about which an agreement has already been reached:

- The Inter-American Convention against Corruption "Inter American Convention against Corruption" of 1996.

- The Organization for Economic Cooperation and Development "Organization for Economic Cooperation Development" (OECD) of 1998.

- The 1999 Civil-Law Convention against Corruption of the Council of Europe.

- The EU Convention on the protection of the EU's financial interests of 1995 and the two protocols on public corruption.

- The European Union Convention for the fight against bribery of EC officials or officials of Member States of 1997.

- Common European Union provisions against corruption in the private sector in 1998.

- The provisions regarding police and judicial cooperation in criminal matters; the art. 29 of the Treaty on European Union.

- The United Nations Convention against Corruption adopted in October 2003 by the UN Assembly."

Before the globalization of information, every people was attentive to their acts or state of corruption in an isolated struggle.

Today, thanks to telematics, the perception of acts and the state of corruption is globalized, sensitively increasing the resentment of the excluded.

It is time for governments to act, before resentment turns into a world conflict, because law does not fill belly and where there is hunger, necessity dulls reason.

CHAPTER 3

Intervention of International Law by Anti-Corruption Conventions

We deem it fundamental to combat corruption that the society is the passive subject of the infringement.

Professor Antonio Beristain (2000: 127) in commenting on the Declaration on Fundamental Principles of justice for victims of crime and abuse of power, underpins the victimization of the Administration State by corruption:

> "Victims" shall mean persons who, individually or collectively, have suffered damage, including physical or mental injury, emotional distress, financial loss and substantial impairment of their fundamental rights, as a result of acts or omissions that violate legislation in force in the Member States, including that which condemns the abuse of power."

Between 1997 and 2007 seven regional or international agreements related to the fight against corruption were adopted, as the INTERPOL[3] website reveals:

"Convenios en materia de lucha contra la corrupción"

Convenio	Acrónimo	Adopción / Signatarios / Rati caciones	Entrada en vigor	Abierto a	Enlace al texto del convenio
Convención Interameri-cana contra la Corrupción	*OEA*	*Do.*	*6 de marzo de 1997*	*Estados miem-bros de la Organización de los Estados Americanos (34 Estados, salvo Cuba, que es miembro de la OEA pero cuya participación está vetada desde 1962), y posibilidad de adhesión de cualquier otro Estado.*	*Convención Interameri-cana contra la Corrupción*
Convenio de la OCDE sobre la lucha contra la corrupción	*OCDE*	*Adoptado: 17 de diciembre de 1997 Rati caciones y adhesiones: 36.*	*15 de febrero de 1999*	*Los 30 países de la OCDE y 6 países que no son miembros (Argentina, Brasil, Bul-garia, Chile, Eslovenia y Estonia). Se están estudiando otras solicitudes de adhesión.*	*Convenio de la OCDE sobre la lucha contra la corrupción de los agen-tes públicos extranjeros en las tran-sacciones comerciales internacio-nales*

Convenio penal sobre corrupción del Consejo de Europa	CoE (Crim.)	Adoptado: 4 de noviembre de 1998, por el Consejo de Ministros Signatarios: 48 (a 5 de febrero de 2007) Compuesto por 44 países miembros y 4 países no miembros Rati caciones y adhesiones: 35 (a 5 de febrero de 2007)	1 de julio de 2002	Todos los Estados miembros del Consejo de Europa y 6 países no miembros (Belarús, Canadá, EE.UU., Japón, México y la Santa Sede). Se puede invitar a incorporarse a los Estados miembros de la UE y otros Estados.	Convenio penal sobre corrupción del Consejo de Europa

3 *http://www.interpol.int/Public/Corruption/Conventions/defaultES.asp.*
Aceso em 23.09.11

Convención de las Naciones Unidas contra la Delincuencia Organizada Transnacional	UNTOC	Adoptada: 15 de noviembre de 2000, por la Asamblea General de las Naciones Unidas Signatarios: 147 (a 14 de septiembre de 2007) Rati caciones: 131 (a 5 de febrero de 2007)	29 de septiembre de 2003	Todos los países y organizacio-nes económicas regionales	Convención de Palermo

Convenio civil sobre corrupción del Consejo de Europa	CoE (Civil)	Adoptado: 4 de noviembre de 1999 Signatarios: 41 (a 5 de febrero de 2007), incluidos dos Estados no miembros. Rati caciones y adhesiones: 27 (a 5 de febrero de 2007)	1 de noviembre de 2003	Estados miembros del Consejo de Europa; Estados no miembros que participaron en la redacción del proyecto; otros Estados no miembros previa invitación.	Convenio civil sobre corrupción del Consejo de Europa
Convención de las Naciones Unidas contra la Corrupción	CNUCC	Adoptada: 31 de octubre de 2003, por la Asamblea General de las Naciones Unidas Signatarios: 140 Rati caciones y adhesiones: 98 (a 14 de septiembre de 2007)	14 de diciembre de 2005	Todos los países y organizaciones económicas regionales	Convención de las Naciones Unidas contra la Corrupción
Convención de la Unión Africana para prevenir y combatir la corrupción	UA	Adoptada: 11 de julio de 2003 Signatarios: 40 (a 15 de febrero de 2007) Ratificaciones: 16 (a 15 de febrero de 2007)	4 de agosto de 2006	Estados miembros de la Unión Africana (53)	Convención de la Unión Africana para prevenir y combatir la corrupción

All these instruments recognize that corruption is an international and cross-border phenomenon and express a high level of common political commitment to end this scourge both individually and collectively. Each text establishes an international or regional regulatory and normative framework that facilitates international cooperation, provides a checklist for government reform, establishes the basis for governments to supervise each other and represents a tool for society groups. civilians ask their governments for responsibilities."

3.1 - Comparative study on the existence of unified legislation to combat crimes against public administration and administrative-disciplinary norms on deviations of functional conduct in the EU and NAFTA

Investigating the treaties on the EU - European Union and NAFTA - North American Free Trade Agreement as a paradigm for Mercosur, we realize that these blocs are established as a Treaty or Trade Agreement with some agricultural or customs unified rules, without there being penal legislation and administrative-disciplinary measures dealing with crimes against those Public Administrations.

- European Union:

As an example of unified policy and legislation in specific areas, we mention what happened with the European Union[4] since the Treaty of Lisbon[5] signed by States Parties of the EU on 13 December 2007, with entry into force on 1 December 2009:

"1 - Common Agricultural Policy;

2 - Common Fisheries Policy;

3 - Common criminal interpretation by the Court of Justice of the European Union6, the supreme court of the European Union with jurisdiction over matters of interpretation of European legislation, in particular:

European Commission's accusations against a Member State about non-implementation of a Community directive or other legal obligation.

Accusations by the Member States against the European Commission for exceeding its authority.

Requests from the national courts of EU Member States to clarify the meaning of a specific piece of Community legislation. Those applications are known as references for a preliminary ruling. The Union has many languages and political interests that are not always convergent, and as a consequence, local courts often have difficulty deciding the meaning of a specific law in a given context. The Court will give its opinion, which may or may not clarify the matter, and return the case to the national court. In the context of the references for a preliminary ruling, the Court has jurisdiction only to assist in the interpretation of the law and not in deciding the facts of the dispute at the national level.

> 4 - European Central Bank (ECB): responsible for the Eurozone single currency;
>
> 5 - Joint Defense: Treaty provides for the European Security and Defense Policy to create a common EU defense agreement if the European Council (the leaders) have resolved to do so in a single whereas all Member States give their approval through their normal constitutional procedures;
>
> 6 - "Public Prosecutor" for a limited number of crimes, at the request of 9 Member States."

A group of Spanish and Argentine lawyers under the supervision of David Baigun and Nicolas Garcia Rivas (2006: 8) carried out research on criminal prevention in the European Union and Mercosur and drew valuable conclusions, pointing out gaps of criminalization in the scope of European Union and Mercosur, as follow:

> "International prevention is addressed by professors Riquert and Valeije Alvarez in Latin America and the European Union, respectively. The first one analyzes the Inter-American Convention against Corruption, which establishes criminal penalization mandates for the states, although the aforementioned author

warns of the defective application that is being carried out, without forgetting the gap that represents his disregard for corruption. private, for whose classification proposes as a model the United Nations Convention. For her part, Professor Valeije Alvarez elaborates extensively on the instruments adopted in the European Union against economic crime and its intersection with regard to the prevention of corruption. The author emphasizes that the problem began as an internal or budgetary issue of the Union's own agencies, to be considered from a general point of view or, if preferred, from the different Member States; However, there is no need in his opinion for the necessary debate on the different criminal figures or on the effective harmonization of infractions and sanctions in the European sphere. To its reconstruction the author dedicates suggestive doctrinal lines. In the same vein, the presentation by Professor and Judge Sáez Capel indicates that the classification of corruption in the private sector suffers from a rigorous analysis of the protected legal right. The Framework Decision of the Council on corruption in the private sector is analyzed in its work and the existence of gaps in this respect in the MERCOSUR legal systems is emphasized."

- NAFTA:

With regard to NAFTA, reading in Article 102 of the Treaty leads us to believe, *ab initio,* that it is not the purpose of its signatories to unite laws relating to crimes against public administration and standards of conduct for public officials. Here is the text of the mentioned article:

"Article 102: Objectives

1. The objectives of this Treaty, developed more specifically through its principles and rules, including those of national treatment, most favored nation treatment and transparency, are the following:

(a) eliminate barriers to trade and facilitate the cross-border movement of goods and services between the territories of the Parties;

(b) promote conditions of fair competition in the free trade zone;

(c) substantially increase investment opportunities in the territories of the Parties;

(d) protect and enforce, in an adequate and effective manner, the intellectual property rights in the territory of each of the Parties;

(e) create effective procedures for the application and compliance with this Treaty, for its joint administration and for the resolution of controversies; Y

(f) establish guidelines for further trilateral, regional and multilateral cooperation aimed at expanding and improving the benefits of this Agreement.

2. The Parties shall interpret and apply the provisions of this Agreement in the light of the objectives set forth in paragraph 1 and in accordance with the applicable rules of international law."

It is recorded that under the laws of the United States, the NAFTA treaty more closely approximates a congressional-executive agreement than a treaty, as can be seen from the "Exceptions" provided for in Chapter XXI, Part Eight, article 2101.

3.2 - International anti-corruption conventions

There is no more detailed "manual" of fighting corruption in the history of mankind than the Inter-American Convention against Corruption (IACAC), followed by the United Nations Convention Against Corruption (UNCAC), which is why we will focus on the study of these two sources of international law, as efficient guns to combat corruption and as a legal paradigm to propose the unification of the penal law, procedural and administrative-disciplinary legislation of Mercosur.

We will not focus on Mercosur integration. We propose to take a step forward with the unification of the criminal, procedural and administrative-disciplinary legislation of the crimes and acts of improbity practiced by public officials against the Mercosur Public Administrations.

With so many texts of international law dealing with the fight against corruption, it is clear that the ifficacy of the law will come from its application and not from its existence.

How to guarantee the efficacy of the fight against corruption? To do so, the IACAC recommends introducing its rules into the internal order of each country.

If the internal combat can be effective, as it has been prooved in some Countries like New Zealand, Denmark, Finland, Norway, Switzerland and Singapore (this one was one the most corrupt until 1950s), will not it be even more so if countries within the same bloc unify their anti-corruption legislation? These and other answers can be found in the chapters that follow.

David Baigun and Nicolas Garcia (2006: 129) legally synthesized the IACAC into administrative and criminal measures against corruption, as follows:

Gráficamente la Convención podría sintetizare en

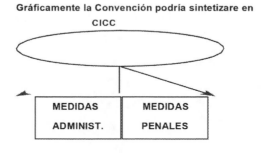

We present below a comparative study on the ratification, interpretation, symmetry and application in the internal legal order of Mercosur, through the tables that we elaborate.

3.2.1 - Table 1 - Inter-American Convention against Corruption (IACAC) - Signature and ratification

Argentina	Brasil	Paraguai	Uruguai	Venezuela
Signed:29.03.96 Rati each:29.03.96	Signed: 29.03.96 Rati each:10.07.02	Signed:29.03.96 Rati each:29.11.96	Signed: 29.03.96 Rati each:28.10.98	Signed: 29.03.96 Rati each:22.05.97

3.2.2 - Table 2 - Literal interpretation of the IACAC by the Organization of American States (OAS)

Concerned by the signatories of the CICC	It is established by the signatories of the CICC	Propose as Principles for Combating Corruption
The ever closer links between corruption and the proceeds of illicit trafficking in drugs, which threaten and erode legitimate commercial and financial activities and society at all levels;	That corruption undermines the legitimacy of public institutions and attacks society, the moral order and justice, as well as against the integral development of peoples;	- International cooperation between the States
That corruption is often one of the instruments used to deal with organized crime in order to achieve its goals;	That representative democracy, an indispensable condition for the stability, peace and development of the region, requires, by its own nature, the fight against all forms of corruption in the exercise of public functions and acts of corruption specifically linked to their exercise;	- Responsibilities of all States;

Cases of corruption that penetrate various sectors of society, which may jeopardize a significant proportion of States' resources and threaten political stability and sustainable development;	That the fight against corruption strengthens democratic institutions and avoids disruptions in the economy, vices in public management and deterioration of social morality;	– Awareness of the existence and seriousness of corruption
	The importance of generating an awareness among the population of the countries of the region of the existence and seriousness of this problem and of the need to strengthen the participation of civil society in preventing and combating corruption;	– The need to strengthen the involvement of civil society in preventing and combating corruption;
	QueThat corruption, in some cases, is of international importance, which requires a coordinated action by States to combat it and to do so;	– Responsibility of all State Members
	The need to adopt as soon as possible an international instrument to promote and facilitate international cooperation to combat corruption and, in particular, to take appropriate action against persons committing acts of corruption in the exercise of the public functions or specifically related to that exercise, as well as with respect to assets resulting from those acts	– Prevention and detection of corruption
		– Punishment and eradication of corruption

3.2.3 - Table 3 - UNCAC - United Nations Convention against Corruption - Signature and ratification

Argentina	Brasil	Paraguai	Uruguai	Venezuela
Signed: 10.12.03 Rati each: 28.08.06	Signed: 09.12.03 Rati each: 15.06.05	Signed: 09.12.03 Rati each: 1.06.05	Signed: 09.12.03 Rati each: 10.01.07	Signed: 10.12.03 Rati each: 08.03.07

3.2.4 - Table 4 — Literal interpretation of UNCAC by UN

It is a concern of the signatories	It is established by the signatories	Propose as Principles for Combating Corruption
The seriousness of the problems and threats posed by corruption, to the stability and security of societies, by weakening the institutions and values of democracy, ethics and justice, and by compromising sustainable development and the rule of law;	That corruption has ceased to be a local problem in order to become a transnational phenomenon affecting all societies and economies, international cooperation is needed to prevent and fight against it	- Substantive due process of law in criminal proceedings and in civil or administrative procedures relating to property rights;
The links between corruption and other forms of crime, in particular organized crime and economic corruption, including money laundering;	That the availability of technical assistance can play an important role so that States are better able to prevent and combat corruption, including by strengthening their capacities and creating institutions;	- Responsibilities of all Member States and that they should cooperate with each other, with the support and participation of individuals and groups not belonging to the public sector, such as civil society, non-governmental organizations and community-based organizations, so that their efforts in this area are and cazes;

Cases of corruption that penetrate various sectors of society, which may jeopardize a significant proportion of States' resources and threaten political stability and sustainable development;	That illicit personal enrichment can be particularly harmful to democratic institutions, national economies and the rule of law;	– Management of public affairs and goods; – Equity; – Responsibility; – Equality before the law; – Need to preserve integrity and foster a culture of rejection of corruption.

With the signing of the UN Convention against Corruption, States Parties undertake to comply with their provisions and become liable to pressure and even economic sanctions by the international community.

In Brazil, the UN Convention against Corruption was ratified by Legislative Decree No. 348 of May 18, 2005, and promulgated by Presidential Decree No. 5,687, dated January 31, 2006.

The signing and ratification of the Treaties lies in the free manifestation of their adherence by the parties to the common good.

It is in this context that we introduce the idea of unifying anti-corruption legislation of Mercosur as a paradigm for other economic blocs. We believe that this action depends only on the existence of political and juridical will, since we have been able to prove the symmetries existing in Mercosur's legal systems.

The proposal to unify criminal law, procedural and administrative-disciplinary law has a number of constitutional foundations that favor it, in view of the fact that the the member countries of Mercosur have the following similarities in their standard legislation:

1 – Republican Form of government (The Political System);

2 – Presidentialism as system of government;

3 - Organic-functional structure of Public Administration; and

4 – Defined system of crimes against Public Administrations, as shown in the following Synoptic Table.

3.2.5 - Table 5 - Symmetry between State, Government, Public Administration, crimes against Public Administration, criminal prosecution and special procedure for judging crimes of public officials, in the legislation of members of Mercosur

Structure of Constitutional Powers	Holder of Criminal Action	Structure of the Public Administration (AP)	Crimes against public administration	Special Procedures for the Judgment of Crimes of Public Officials
Similar in all countries, with the exception of Venezuela that has 05 powers (highlighting the Electoral Power and Citizen Power)	Similar: The Public Prosecution is the dominus litis of criminal action.	Similar: it is divided into Direct and Indirect, Centralized or Decentralized, with the Chief of the Presidency of the Republic, assisted by its Ministers of State.	Similar: The structured pipelines are identical only by changing the nomenclature of the criminal type, by virtue of the language: • Bribe or Tip; • Nepotism; • Extortion; • Traffic of influence in the Public Administration; • Use of private government information for people or friends or relatives;	Only Brazil has a specific chapter on the prosecution of crimes committed by public officials. In Brazil, for example, crimes are tried by courts of law and the official has the right to a prior defense before criminal
Source: National Constitution	Source: Criminal Procedure Code -CPP	Source: Organic Laws of Public Administration		

28

			• Purchase and sale of judicial decisions; • Receipt of gifts or bribes; • Active Corruption • Passive Corruption • Smuggling facilitation or tax evasion • Embezzlement • Extorsion practiced by public officials • Prevarication Source: Penal Code	proceedings are instituted. Source: Procedural code penal

3.2.6 - UNCAC - United Nations Convention against Corruption

In the context of international law, the UNCAC is a sign of a general rule to be obeyed by the signatory countries in the fight against corruption, including public officials, not objecting to or suggesting the unification of national laws, as can be seen from the text that we transcribe:

"Codes of conduct for public officials

(...)

4. Each State Party shall also consider, in accordance with the fundamental principles of its domestic law, the possibility of establishing measures and systems to facilitate public officials to report any acts of corruption to the competent authority when they are aware of them in the exercise of their functions.

5. Each State Party shall endeavor, when and in accordance with the fundamental principles of its domestic law, to establish measures and systems to require public officials to make statements to the competent authorities regarding, inter alia, their external

activities and with jobs, investments, assets and gifts or important benefits that may give rise to a conflict of interests regarding their attributions as public servants."

Older than the UNCAC is the Inter-American Convention against Corruption (IACAC), which in its article II and items provides as mission of its signatories:

"1. Promote and strengthen the development, by each State Party, of the mechanisms necessary to prevent, detect, punish and eradicate corruption; and

2. To promote, facilitate and regulate cooperation among States Parties to ensure the effectiveness of measures and actions taken to prevent, detect, punish and eradicate corruption in the exercise of public functions, as well as acts of corruption specifically linked to its exercise."

The excerpts we underline demonstrate the Respect Reservation by International Conventions by national legal systems, since they do not suggest the union of national legislations, mainly because they are supranational conventions and not regional blocs of nations.

3.2.7 - International Conventions on money laundering

There are four International Conventions dealing with the fight against money laundering:

1 - Vienna Convention, 1988;

2 - Convention for the Suppression of the Financing of Terrorism, adopted in 1999;

3 - Palermo Convention against Transnational Organized Crime, 2000; and

4 - Merida Convention against Corruption, December 2003.

We take article 4 of the Palermo Convention as an example of protection of national sovereignty:

"Article 4

Protection of sovereignty

1. States Parties shall comply with their obligations under this Convention in accordance with the principles of sovereign equality and the territorial integrity of States as well as non-interference in the internal affairs of other States.

2. Nothing in this Convention shall entitle any State Party to exercise, in the territory of another State, jurisdiction or functions which the domestic law of that State rests exclusively with its authorities."

The States Parties of the Palermo Convention signal a global policy to combat the laundering of illicit assets arising from various kinds of crimes, including crimes committed by public officials, which imply an annual deviation of over US $200 billion only in Brazil, while The Organisation for Economic Co-operation and Development (OECD) says that corruption deviates about US$ 2 trilhões, the equivalent to all the GDP of France.

To combat the laundering of illicit assets arising from various kinds of crimes is a way of preserving probity in the Public Administration and channeling more money into social programs, which are important to strengthening democracy.

CHAPTER 4

A Comparative Study on Italian Administrative Justice and Brazilian Administrative Justice that may Serve as Paradigm for Mercosur

Comparing is an inherent activity of being thinking. One of the earliest and most new ways of knowing and transmitting knowledge was the philosophical empiricism.

It was observing and imitating that, in theory, man was first charmed with knowledge. Early in life he learned that repetition is the mother of learning.

Greek philosophers such as Socrates and his most expressive disciples are quick to believe that contemplation was a mission.

Aristotle would not have developed his principle of "non-contradiction" without the power of observation, because it is it that leads man to establish comparison between the thing that cannot be and be, at the same time.

Whatever this observable Aristotelian "thing", which is certainly not the same Roman "res", it would have to be observed and questioned to exhaustion so that one could arrive at the understanding of the "excluded third."

In all sciences, there is a truth to be pursued. In Comparative Law one relevant question is how to apprehend knowledge to establish closer comparisons of legal truth.

Apprehend one truth is not the same thing that "learn a truth". It is is intercept, bring it to you, arrest and chain the truth in your knowledge by exhaustive reflexions. An ordinary being learn relatively easily something by memorizing it, but the one who loves knowlegde reflect about it and more than other thing doubt it!

Plato advises in his book "The Republic" that one does not learn by answering but by asking.

In this line of reasoning, Aristotle was in charge of developing the questions of knowledge. What, how, where, when, why, for what, who. These seven questions can be decisive for the knowledge of the observed object.

This is why the activity of comparison can be accepted as inherent to rational being and constitutes one of the main ways of identifying the attributes of the observed object.

In this way, the comparative study of Law becomes an efficient method for the identification of paradigms that can serve the legal operator, whether in the European Union, NAFTA, Mercosur or another block of nations, that aims to integrate or unite.

Economic integration is a reality in the world. Unification, on the other hand, is an area that is still underdeveloped, but not virgin, since the eighteenth century the Politics and Law, advocate feelings of belonging to all nations to a "universal family," as if derives, for example, from the Universal Declaration of Human Rights of 1789, which provides that society is one body. Here is the preambular excerpt on the theme:

> "The representatives of the French People, formed into a National Assembly, considering ignorance, forgetfulness or contempt of the rights of man to be the only causes of public misfortunes and the corruption of Governments, have resolved to set forth, in a solemn Declaration, the natural, unalienable and sacred rights of man, to the end that this Declaration, constantly present to all members of the body politic, may remind them unceasingly of their rights and their duties; to the end that the acts of the legislative power and those of the executive power, since they may be continually compared with the aim of every political institution, may thereby be the more respected; to the end that the demands of the citizens, founded henceforth on simple and incontestable principles, may always be directed toward the maintenance of the Constitution and the happiness of all."

Along the same path follows the Universal Declaration of Human Rights, UN of 1948:

"Preamble

Whereas recognition of the inherent dignity and of the equal and inalienable rights of all members of the human family is the foundation of freedom, justice and peace in the world,"

If we are all members of this social body of the state we want to qualify as a family, the attractiveness of the Law is that we do not practice autophagy, attacking us to achieve benefits against others. Thomas Hobbes in his book Leviathan explains about that as well (2011: 95):

"Thus there are three main causes of contention in human nature: competition, misery, and glory. The competition forces men to attack each other to gain some benefit, the detachment assures them of safety and glory, reputation. The first cause leads men to use violence to get hold of the staff, the wife, the livestock and the livestock of other men; the second leads them to use violence to defend these assets; the third makes them resort to force for insignificant reasons, such as a word, a smile, a scorn, an opinion

Different from his or any other sign of direct underestimation of his person, or that rests with his friends, his nation, his profession, or the name of his family."

In the area of international law, the Conventions and Agreements try to model National Law in order to raise the feeling of "universal family" that preserv itself and work together, for the development of each of its members and, consequently, of the entire society.

In view of the above, we consider it appropriate to insert in this chapter 4 a brief comparative study of Italian Administrative Justice and Brazilian Administrative Justice, considering that we have a paradigm of administrative justice with _una lex una jurisdictio_, which can be another tool to help fight against corruption in Mercosur and in the world.

4.1 - The Brazilian Administrative Law System

A system can be lexically conceptualized as a set of parts that converge to a whole.

For our part, we assume the loose relativism that the "whole" to which the parts converge will always be part of another "whole."

For example, the universe is composed of parts that interact, without reaching the "absolute whole". In the same way Man is a bio-psychological system composed of parts that interact and whose "absolute whole" science still not know.

So too the Law is a set of different parts that interact in a "whole." Each State has its legal system, its "whole". This national law has evolved into what we now call Community law in the integrated communities of states, such as NAFTA (North American Free Trade Agreement), Mercosur, European Union and, part of the International Law system that guides all other spheres of government in the world.

Each State of this international community is responsible for the solution of its internal conflicts, as a way of preserving the general peace, as proclaims the criminal principle of Cosmopolitan Justice, which says the crime should be punished wherever it occurs to prevent it from becoming a pandemic that affects the community of nations.

Yet it is necessary to understand that it is not the world that changes but man and this new anthropocentric man wants the political dignity that formal democracy has promised through the Democratic Rule of Law and has not delivered. This is why the community of nations has decided to create means for the prevention and repression of corruption.

If the prevention and repression of crime follows its course of undeniable importance, it seems relevant to us to consider the extremely usefulness of Administrative Law as a tool of cognoscence for the realization of collective needs, in the figure of the State Administration. We cannot forget that each Public Administration of each State is destined to provide the public services to each and every citizen.

This same Public Administration, which has gained a body by its organs, entities and public officials, is the object of study of Administrative Law in all systems of Civilistic Tradition, in Common law and even regimes of exception or dictatorials because not even dictators escape to serve people in certain ammount.

Eventhoug the progress, the system of world administrative law is still a political-legal body in formation. Setting the time frame of its appearing is hard.

Some institutes fo Administrative Law have records in pre-classic antiquity, such as edicts, the organization of cities, public functions, investiture and dismissal in public functions, forms of petition to the public authorities, treatment of corrupt assets and liabilities, Concessions and Permissions given to traders or religious temples. That's why is hard to trace its timeline.

The systemic study of the State seems to be a little bit more new, since, it is the opinion of many historians that we owe the audacity and adventure of developing the theory of the state to the Greeks, like the pre-Socratic Tales of Miletus around seventh and sixth centuries before commom Era. Tales of Miletus, for example, was famous for its struggle to unite the Cities-States of Asia Minor, a task which certainly requires some knowledge of Law and Politics.

The fact that Aristotle had studied 153 Constitutions of Greek City-States, to write his work "Politics" is symptomatic not only of the antiquity existence of a systemic comparative study, but also of the political-juridical systematization of the State.

The government of the ancient Greek cities was composed of the borned citizens, who met in the public squares to deliberate and decide their fate, by means of Political-Administrative rules.

Older still are the historical records of Egyptian civilization, which point to the fact that Pharaohs had the leading role in the creation of laws, "although no one has yet found a Code of Egyptian Laws, as has happened with Code of Hammurabi "(in Mário Curtis Giordani, in History of Eastern Antiquity, ed. Vozes, 10th ed., 1997).

These political-administrative laws governed the conduct of society under various known aspects of the time, through administrative impositions such as the payment of tribute for the costing of military forces, the construction of cylinders for the storage of crops, including the financing of the popular lace races of chariots, theater and later the games in the arenas of fight, among other public or private activities the States fostered.

The distribution of the Egyptian social strata, thirty-two centuries before commom Era, according to Maria Januaria Vilela Santos (in General History, Attica, pp. 36-42), included the class of nobles or officials in charge of the administration of kingdom, among them Joseph who came to be the second in line and who biblically, is considered the "savior" of Egypt.

Joseph's story in Egypt and the food storage in the time of the "lean cows" show the concern and the oldness of the state's policy of Regulation of minimum stocks, a practice that has been in force up to now, as in the case of Brazilian Politics of Regulation of Minimum Energy Stock, regulated by ANP Resolution No. 67, DE 9.12.2011 - DOU 13.12.2011 - rectified DOU 16.12.2011, which states:

> "Considering Law No. 12,490, of September 16, 2011, which amends art. 8 of Law No. 9,478, of August 6, 1997, establishing that the ANP may require regulated agents to maintain minimum stocks of biofuels, as well as guarantees and proof of capacity to serve the biofuels market;"

The law will continue its course of change, but the policy of minimum stock of provisions came to stay and that happens because modern States know the importance of the multi-year planning.

In the Platonic and Aristotelian records we find embryonic institutes of Administrative Law. Aristotle, for instance, said:

> "A family supplies itself better than an individual, and a state even better than a family. Now the State is an association of men capable of supplying their existence "(in Politics, Ed. Martin Claret, and page 39)."

For the Administration State to respond to the needs of its citizens, it needs to integrate the political-juridical spheres into a "whole" capable of meeting the minimum needs of its members through the provision of its set of institutions, public officials and by partnership with third sector and others.

One of the universal and best examples of administrative organization is found in Jewish writings, most notably in the Book of Exodus, in which management principles such as Planning, Coordination, Control, Delegation of Competence, and Decentralization are evidenced.

Let us look at the biblical account:

"Chapter 18

1 Now Jethro, the priest of Midian, the father-in-law of Moses, heard all that God had done to Moses and Israel his people, as the LORD had brought Israel out of Egypt.

2 And Jethro, Moses' father-in-law, took Zipporah, the wife of Moises, after he had sent her...

13 And it came to pass on the other day, that Moses sat down to judge the people; and the people stood before Moses from morning until evening.

14 And when Moses' father-in-law saw all that he did to the people, he said, "What is this that you do to the people? Why do you sit down alone, and all the people stand before you from morning till evening?

15 And Moses said to his father-in-law, it is because this people come to me to inquire of God;

16 When he has any business, come to me, that I may judge between one and another, and declare to you the statutes of God and his laws.

17 And Moses' father in law said unto him, It is not good that thou doest.

18 Thou shalt utterly faint, so shalt thou be like this people that are with thee; because this business is very difficult for you; you just cannot do it.

19 Hear now my voice, I will counsel thee, and God shall be with thee. Be thou for the people before God, and thou bear the causes of God;

20 And declare unto them the statutes and the laws, and declare unto them the way in which they must walk, and the work, which they are to do.

21 And thou of all the people seek out able men, fearful of God, men of truth, that hate avarice; and put them upon them by the chiefs of a thousand, the majors of a hundred, the majors of fifty, and the majors of ten;

22 That they may judge this people at all times; and let any serious business bring you, but any small business they deem it; so shall you relieve yourself of the burden, and they shall carry it with you.

23 If this be done, and God commanded it, then you shall be able to stand; so all this people in peace will go to their place.

24 And Moses hearkened unto the voice of his father in law, and did all that he had spoken;

25 And Moses chose able men out of all Israel, and put them to the heads of the people; major ones of a thousand, majors of a hundred, majors of fifty and majors of ten.

26 And they have judged the people at all times; the arduous business brought to Moses, and all little business judged them ..."

Note that Jethro, the father-in-law, made Moses realize the misconception of his centralizing leadership. So, what was a bureaucratic administrative machine has been transformed into a paradigm of efficiency for centuries to come. The services were delivered efficiently and effectively. All this happens because Jethro questioned Moses's method. Pay attention to the Jethro's intelligentsia:

Jethro asks:

- Why do you want to decide everything by yourself? (Verse 14)

Jethro affirms:

- Governing is not a task for one person (Verse 18)

Jethro advises:

1 - Declares the statutes and the laws.

2 - Make known to them the way in which they must walk.

3 - Let them know the work which they are to do.

4 – Search for capable men.

5 - Seek honest me.

6 - Decentralizes power (puts them to rule over majors of a thousand, majors of a hundred, majors of fifty, and majors of ten).

7 - Establishes a hierarchical system over them.

If you do not show prejudice with the biblical example, simply because it belongs to a religious book and, instead, priviledge the administration science lessons, certalinly you can say like Archimedes when exclaimed "Heureka! Heureka", you too can say "I have found it". Because what Jethro did was pure science and this is still used up to date in all cycles of public and private sector of global economy.

Moses listened to his father-in-law's advice and the result of this hierarchical system combined with the principles of planning, coordination, control, competence delocalization and decentralization is known and studied around the world up to date.

With so many examples of intervenience of institutes of the Administrative Law in antiquity, as we have listed, I think saying It arose in the eighteenth century after commom Era, as some scholars do is a great historical naivity.

We prefer to believe that Administrative Law follows the steps of social evolution, arriving in Brazil first with a European vocation, and after, in the middle of the twentieth century approaching the Common Law, always in the search of delivering efficient public services, as requires the national legal order, as foreseen in Decree-Law no. 227/1967, Law 9,784 / 99 and the Federal Constitution of 1988.4.1.1 - Schools that contributed to the systematization of Brazilian administrative law

4.1.1 - Schools that have contributed to the systematization of the Brazilian Administrative Law

I feel it is important clarify that the term "school" is used in this encyclopedia as an ideological stream of creators or systematizers of knowledge.

SCHOOL OF FRENCH LAW: It was in 1819 that the Administrative Law was introduced as a university subject in France and was recognized in 1873 as a science endowed with object, method, institutes, principles and its own legal regime. To this school, Brazil has read, without, however, despising the power of transformation of the study compared with the Law of other peoples.

Sylvia Di Pietro quoting José Cretella Júnior in the Treaty of Administrative Law - 1970), says that the autonomy of the Administrative Law came from the famous Blanco case, which occurred in 1873, involving the girl Agnès Blanco who crossing a street in Bordeaux, and the torts she suffered after hit by a wagon that transported raw material between two buildings from the National Tobacco Manufacturing Company.

On that occasion, Counselor David of the Court of Conflicts gave his vote, setting aside the Napoleonic Code and calling for the first time the equation and resolution of the civil responsibility of the State.

The Councilor David, enthusiastic about the case, concluded that the State Council was competent to decide, since the State was part of the legal relationship, making this decision the leading case of civil liability of the State.

In 1945, the French Council of State invoked for the first time, and expressly, its knowledge of the administrative principles for the settlement of the conflicts between the Public Administration and the people.

SCHOOL OF GERMAN LAW: In German law there was no separation of Administrative and Civil Law, as occurred in France. However, Germany credits to itself the systematization of the Administrative Law.

SCHOOL OF ANGLO-AMERICAN LAW: The contribution of English law to the systematization of Brazilian administrative law is undeniable, especially by the decision on the basis of equity and, more modernly, by the creation of special State Agencies, as policy of regulation public and private sector of economy like minning, energy, water, environment, aviation, etc.

In this historical abstract (it is not the focus of this work to historicize the Administrative Law schools) we recall that the Brazilian Administrative Law as a university subject was introduced in 1856 at the São Paulo Law School.

With the 1934 Constitution, in which the State's role in the social and economic spheres is reviewed and expanded, this branch of public law undergoes a significant evolution. Still, it was with the Constitution of October 5, 1988 that it gained its own chapter in the national political-juridical order.

The field of coverage of Brazilian Administrative Law shrinks and expands to the exact extent of ruling political thinking. If economical and political vision is linked to neo-liberal thougths, so we turn to the minimal state and It contracts and if the economical and political vision turn to a socialist state its range of action expands.

4.1.2 - Concept of administrative law

The Brazilian authors adopt several criterias to conceptualize Administrative Law. Among these criterias there is the "Public Service", the "Executive Branch", "Juridical Relations", the "Teleological" criteria, the "Negative or Residual" criteria".

However, in any of the criterias used it cannot be overlooked that Administrative Law is:

- **A science,** because it consists of a body of systematized knowledge which, acquired through observation, identification, research and explanation of certain categories of phenomena and facts, formulated methodically and rationally.

- **A set of principles and rules**. Principles because these are foundations for the construction of the rules governing the relationship between the Administration State and the administered ones.

- **A branch of public law**, because the relations covered by it are of social and collective relevance. Its principles are publicists, since they aim at the promotion and protection of public and non-private interests, which is why the supremacy of the public interest over private interests prevails.

- **A discipline focused in study the Public Administration in all its relations** with the citizens. Under the positive system, it has to strictly obey the law in order to achieve the national development, and under the subjective criteria or point of view, the Administrative Law studies the public official, organs and entities and their duties to delivery public services.

Despite the above mentioned criteria, the most adopted by Brazilian scholars is the Administrative Criterion that affirms that the Administrative Law is "the harmonious set of legal principles that govern the organs, agents and public activities tending to concretely, directly and immediately, to carry out the tasks desired by the State "as said by Hely Lopes Meirelles.

Thus, in the formulation of the concept or perception of Administrtive Law, four elements stand out:

1 - Public Agents:

2 - Public Bodies;

3 - Public Goods; and

4 - Public Services.

Public bodies and public agents are the subjects of the provision of public services while public goods are part of the State of Administration and must be used as a source of satisfaction for the "common good".

The citizens are the recipients of the state action. It is for their needs that the Public Administration must work, for the supremacy is of the people, not of the state, as Abraham Lincoln said in his Gettysburg address of 1863.

The Constitution of 1988 outlined the lines of the Brazilian social state, determining as the rights of the people education, health, security, work, housing, leisure, social security and all of these rights belong to the people and it is for them that the Administration State works, and it is up to the Administrative Law to study and standardize the best way of rendering public services.

That is why I believe it is necessary to add the citizen to the other objects of study of the Administrative Law, since they are the recipients of public services and have a very strict link to the existence of the public institutions and public officials.

I do not believe that such an understanding would alter the essence of the Administrative Criterion. At the same time, the Public Administration does not exist *per se*, but to provide adequate services to the people.

In fact, Public Administration by its organs, agents and activities will always be the object of Administrative Law, as it is the means to concretize the will of the State, in relation to the needs of its citizens.

We understand that the Brazilian legislator has been moving towards this understanding in establishing the rights and duties of the citizens in relation to the Public Administration.

Note, for example, the text of Law no. 9,784 / 99, the Federal Procedure Code of Administrative Law:

> "Art. 3 The administrator has the following rights to the Administration, without prejudice to others that are assured to him:
>
> I - be treated with respect by the authorities and servants, who shall facilitate the exercise of their rights and the fulfillment of their obligations;

II - to have knowledge of the administrative procedures in which he is interested, to have a record of the file, to obtain copies of the documents contained therein and to know the decisions rendered;

III - formulate claims and present documents before the decision, which will be considered by the competent body;

IV - to be assisted, optionally, by a lawyer, except when mandatory representation, by virtue of law.

Art. 4 The duties of the administration before the Administration, without prejudice to others provided for in a normative act:

I - state the facts truthfully;

II - proceed with loyalty, urbanity and good faith;

III - do not act recklessly;

IV - to provide the information requested and to collaborate to clarify the facts."

According to our understanding, the concept of Administrative Law must be reengineered to scope the following elements:

1 - Entities and Public Organs;

2 - Public Agents;

3 - Public Goods;

4 - Public Services;

5 - Litigious legal activity or not; and

6 – The managed or administered ones.

The new the Federal Procedure Code of Administrative Law (Law No. 9.784 / 99) suggests a reordering of the concept of Administrative Law by stating:

> "This Law establishes basic rules on the administrative process in the scope of the Federal Direct and Indirect Administration, protection of the rights of those managed and to the best fulfillment of the functions of the Administration ".

The guarantee that the State must converge to meet the needs of the Administered ones, is expressed in paragraph one of article one, like this:

> "The provisions of this Law also apply to the organs of the Legislative and Judicial Branches of the Union, while performing administrative functions."

Based on what we have studied, we understand Administrative Law as the branch of public law which, due to a contentious or not contentious legal activity, has for object of study public bodies and entities, agents, goods and public services that are intended to serve to the administered ones.

4.1.3 - Other concepts of Administrative Law

In the words of Maria Sylvia Zanella Di Pietro Administrative Law is "the branch of public law that has as its object the organs, agents and administrative juridical persons that integrate the Public Administration, the non-contentious legal activity that it exercises and the assets of which it is used to the attainment of their ends of political nature" (in Administrative Law, 6th ed ed, at 47).

Administrative Law in the words of the always remembered Hely Lopes Meirelles and Diogenes Gasparini is: "The harmonious set of juridical principles that govern the organs, agents and public activities tending to concretely, directly and immediately carry out the goals desired by the State". (In Brazilian Administrative Law, 27th Ed. Malheiros Editores).

4.1.4 - The Brazilian administrative litigation system

We do not apply in our Administrative Law *una lex una jurisdiction* typical of the Judiciary branch, but it is undeniable that our system is both spontaneous and contentious.

It is spontaneous because Public Administration exists with the mission of providing public services and contentious because the citizens may provoque the Public Administration to give them efficient and adequate public services, even by petition to the Judiciary branch.

The administrative conflict is the daily routine of the State-Administration. So, When people requires the creation, modification, transfer or extinction of rights before public bodies or entities and they deny them, the conflict is created, Yet when any of the citizens feels the administration is not doing what has to do, there the conflict is installed and it has to be solved in the federal sphere of the Powers of the Republic, according to the procedure dictated by special processes or according to the law dictated by the Federal Administrative Procedure Code (Law No. 9.784 / 1999).

The solution of the Administrative liltigation shall be solved inside of each organ or institution of the State, but not by the rule of "one law one jurisdiction", because this happens only inside of the Judicial Branch, eventhough both Administrative and Judicial processes are ruled by due process of the law. If any part in the process loses the claim in District Courts they can raise to the Court Appeals and, finally to the Supreme Court.

The Brazilian Federal Procedure Administrative Code establishes appeals until three administraive instances (see article 57 of Law no. 9.784 / 99)

The rule of "one law one jurisdiction" is foreseen in article 5°, item XXXV of 1988 Brazilian Constitution. There is written that "the law shall not exclude from the Judiciary Branch the appreciation of the injury or threat to law".

It must be no forgotten that while the Judiciary branch only acts through provocation (ne procedat judex ex offcio), Public Addmindistration, whose chief in a republican system is a President, must acts spontaneously without any nead of provocation to deliver efficient and adequate public service.

The administrative litigation, be it related to internal issues of the Public Administration of the Powers of the Republic (Legislative, Executive and Judiciary branch, for exemple) or to the relationship between Public Administration in each level of the Republic and the client-citizen is a reality that cannot be denied in the scope of Law.

By way of example, we transcribe one decision of the Brazilian Supreme Court on the existence of litigation in the system of Administrative Law:

"HC 76420 / SP - SÃO PAULO / HABEAS CORPUS / Reporter: Min. MAURÍCIO CORRÊA / Trial: 06/16/1998

Judging Body: Second Class Publication: DJ 14-08- 1998 PP-00004 EMENT VOL-01918-02 PP-00263

HABEAS-CORPUS. CRIME AGAINST THE TAX ORDERS: FRAUD THE TRIBUNAL AUDIT, INSERTING UNEQUAL ELEMENTS, OR IM- NING OPERATION OF ANY KIND IN DOCUMENT OR BOOK REQUIRED BY THE TAX LAW. NUMBERS ALLEGED: MEDIUM INVESTMENT OPENING NEW LOOK AT THE ACCUSATION AFTER THE FINAL CLAIMS OF DEFENSE; NOT PERFORMING THE MANDATORY BODY EXAMINATION OF CRIME; LACK OF COMPREHENSIVE EXAMINATION IN THE JUDGMENT AND JUDGMENT OF THE THESES OF DEFENSE, MAKING THE TWO MARGINS OF THE CONDUCTANCE JUDGMENT TWO OF THE THREE IMPUTED DUTIES, WHICH WOULD BE AUTHORIZED BY THE TAX LEGISLATION.

1. The procedural inversion, speaking before the defense and then the accusation in the national allegations (CPP, article 500, I and III), implies nullity as much as in the case of oral support (RECrim no. 91,661-MG, in RTJ 92/448), for offense to the principle of ample defense and the contradictory. However, when the defense argues a preliminary issue in the domestic claims, it is legitimate to open the hearing and the manifestation of the Public Prosecution Service, both with legal support in the analogical application of art. 327, first part, of the Code of Civil Procedure, as provided for in art. (3) of the Code of Criminal Procedure, since in such a case

it is strictly for the other party to express himself in accordance with the principle of adversary, whose exercise is not a monopoly of defense. 2. The accuser is charged with the burden of proof (CPP, article 156), and the Public Prosecutor's Office must request the examination of a body of offense in the case of an infraction that leaves traces, which can not even be supplied by the con- (CPP, article 158), under penalty of annulment (CPP, article 564, III, b). This standard is to bring to the record an uncontroversial proof of the material existence of the offense, a provision which, however, is necessary when, as in the case, the corpus delicti itself came to the file. Precedents. 3. Allegation of omission in the conviction decision for not having fully examined the theses of the defense, on the grounds that two of the three conduct imputed to the patient could have protection under the tax legislation. Prima facie, the claim is wrecked in paralogism, because if there are three autonomous conducts that typify the same offense, two of them remain, which is sufficient to support the conviction to the minimum sentence applied to the patient. The theses defended by the petitioners in order to justify the typical conduct should have been submitted to administrative or judicial litigation and not exercised by something similar to the arbitrary exercise of their own reasons because, when to the detriment of the crime, by the express expression of the will of the legislator. Moreover, where the decision takes a reasoned argument implicitly, it implicitly removes those which are incompatible with it and there is no need for a full examination of each of those which have not been accepted. 4. Habeas-corpus known, but rejected. "(Emphasis added)

The existence of administrative litigation also functions as a means of vigilance of the ethics in the administrative acts practiced in all instances of government with the following ends:

- Prevention;

- Intervention; and

- Supervision.

The prevention, intervention and supervision of the Ethical action by public officials in relation to the business with private sector of the economy and the needs of the client-citizen is attempt to:

- Avoiding the abuse of power;

- Avoiding deviation of power;

- Avoiding omission in doing the duties;

- Avoiding corruption.

The Administrative litigation manifests itself in different kinds of Adminstrative conflicts, as follows:

- Agrarian conflicts;

- Minning conflicts;

- Environmental conflicts;

- Internal Revenue conflicts;

- Transport system conflicts;

- Housing conflicts;

- Health and Social Security conflicts, etc.

The Brazilian system of Administrative litigation keeps at least five similarities with the Italian system, such as:

1-The recognition that the conflict is inherent in man and therefore inseparable from micro or macro social groups;	2 - The certainty of inadequacy of private revenge as a solution to the conflicts;	3 - The legitimacy of the State and its institutions as the main agent of pacification of social conflicts;	4 - The systematization and organic structuring of the commutative justice of giving to each one what is his and the distributive justice and its proportional equality, associated with the idea of the division and balance of legitimized Constitucionas Powers.	5 - The "confusion" of the formal and of the substantial state of rule, insofar as the words justice, morality and law are merging into a single concept, with the state as the sole provider of such virtues.

The framework of the Roman-Germanic system of Law adopted by Brazil, Mercosur and several countries of the world has advantages and disadvantages in relation to other systems, such as that of the Common Law. A disadvantage is the rigidity of the principle of legality insofar it imposes itself on the equity of a more casuistic interpretation and in accordance with the need of the client-citizen.

As an advantage, we can point out that the positivation or codification adopted by Roman-Germanic system reserves less margin for subjective interpretations, being able to guarantee, based on social consensus, what has been previously defined and agreed as justice.

Thus, as the protection of rights was evoqued by the modern state of rule, the method established for achieving this protection against threat or injury to rights of the client-citizens, lies both in the provocation of the Judiciary branch and in the spontaneous claims made to Executive or Judicial branch. We have discussed a little more deep these themes in our book on Administrative Law.

The scope of judicial protection requires special procedures. The 1988 Brazilian Constitution in its article five, simplifies the classification of processes telling they are of two kinds. you see? They are of only two kinds, administrative and judicial. Let me transcribe the constitucional text for you to see:

"LV - to the litigants, in judicial or administrative process, and to the accused in general are assured the contradictory and ample defense, with means and resources inherent therein";

Therefore, in Brazil judicial process is that one that develops before the Judiciary branch. All others are, in the broad sense, administrative processes.

In a strict sense, the administrative process has the face of the organ or entity in which it is formed and develops, deserving reminding that in Brazil or Italy, Public Administration can be considered as the group of organs and public agents conducive to the provision of public services.

Therefore the administrative justice is the one that applies the administrative jurisdiction to the conflicts between the Public Administration and the clients-citizens and even in absence of conflicts, in case of spontaneous delivery of the public services, insofar this is the essence of the existence of the Public Administration in every country of the world. If it does not it, there is no reason to its existence but to the resistence to it, until other kind of government must be found.

As an example of Brazilian administrative litigation system, imagine that a certain mining company applies for the purpose of exploiting diamonds. All the business operation only can be done under a Federal Union concession, according to constitucional and infraconstitucional law. This is what Brazilian Law requires in accordance to its rigid principle of legality associated to other important constitucionals and infraconstitucionals principles.

Everything must be done according to the law and whithout law nothing can be done. This is a universal mantra repeated in Brazil Administrative fiels that unhappily, seems dead words in facer of the corruption system installed in every instance of the Republic.

The fact is that In any of the stages of the minning, whether in research or in the extracting to sell minerals, if there is a conflict of rights between the Federal Union (represented by minning agency) and private enterprises, the solution will come through by an administrative process in which the due process of law is ensured by up to three instances of appeals with the formation of an Administrative res judicata, or even with the possibility of judicialization of the case, due to the inexistence of the one law one jurisdictio in the Brazilian Administrative Law.

It should be noted that the Brazilian clients-citizens runs the risk of going through an entire administrative crusade, and in spite of that, somtimes have to wait years to see the claims solved. In a plenty of situations the clients-citizens have to judicialize the claims, requiring another legal provision to the Judiciary with his judges and courts.

It is different in the Italian administrative system of law, since it is structured in a double degree of jurisdiction with a specific justice, in which the judged thing occurs only once, as will be seen below.

4.1.5 - Synoptic table of the Brazilian Administrative Law

Executive branch	Legislative branch	Judicial branch
1 - it is based on the provocation of the clients-citizens (litigation) or spontaneity of the provision of public services. 2 - There is no frameworked specific jurisdictional system with specific courts and judges to solve the claims, like it happens in the Judicial branch, although the recent Federal Code of Administrative Procedure (Law No. 9.784 / 1999)	- Same as executive power.	- Same as executive power.

make mention of the existence of up to three administrative instances. These instances are all administrative not judicial. 3. The solution of disputes shall take place in each body and in each case individually or through the intermediary of the competent authorities, except in rare cases by collegiate bodies different of the courts of Judiciary branch.		

4.1.6 - Advantages and disadvantages of the Brazilian Administrative Law

The advantages of the Brazilian administrative system are:	The disadvantages of the Brazilian system are:
1 - Reduced public spending in the absence of the creation and maintenance of administrative courts geographically distributed throughout the national territory. 2 - Possibility, in theory, of more rapid administrative decisions, since they occur in the internal scope of each organ or entity. 3 – In theory, lower degree of political interference insofar as each administrative authority has the power to decide interna corporis.	1 - Lower degree of specialization of the operators of administrative law. 2 - Failure in uniform equity. Nowadays The Advocacy General of the Union and the Court of Auditors of the Union compile their decision dockets to orient organs and entities, in order for them to decide in the same sense. 3 - Asphyxia of the Judiciary branch by the judicialization of administrative processes, implying in bis in idem. Undoubtedly, such a procedure undermines the e ciency in the provision of the protection of justice, when the

4 - Decadential term of impugnation of the administrative acts more extended to the clident-citizen (5 years in Brazil instead of 60 days adopted by other countries), as seen in article 54 of Law 9,784 / 1999.	Constitution promises relative quick decisions: "LXXVIII to all, in the judicial and administrative spheres, are guaranteed the reasonable duration of the process and the means to guarantee the speed of its proceedings." (article 5)

4.2 - The Italian administrative system of law

If Italian Justice really works, it deserves a separate study, but the Italian Constitution of 1948, in creating administrative justice with *one law one jurisdictio*, in theory, seems to have privileged the principle of the effficiency.

This is what Article 113 of the "Costituzione della Repubblica Italiana" provides, which we transcribe literally:

"Contro gli atti della pubblica amministrazione e` sempre ammessa la tutela giurisdizionale dei diritti e degli interessi legittimi dinanzi agli organi di giurisdizione ordinaria o amministrativa

Tale tutela giurisdizionale non puo` essere esclusa o limitata a particolari mezzi di impugnazione o per determinate categorie di atti.

La legge determina quali organi di giurisdizione possono annullare gli atti della pubblica amministrazione nei casi e con gli effetti previsti dalla legge stessa."

So, the Judicial protection of legitimate rights and interests before organs of ordinary or administrative jurisdiction is always admitted against acts of public administration and such judicial protection can not be excluded or limited to particular reasons of appeal or to certain categories of acts.

The complement of the rule is that the law determines which organs of jurisdiction can annul the acts of the public administration in the cases and with the effects foreseen by the law itself.

Under the command of the Constitution, the law has structured the system of Administrative Law so that the Italian administrative justice is provided within the internal body of each body and entity.

Italy has structured its Administrative Justice in the manner of the functioning of the Brazilian Judiciary branch, with one law one jurisdiction in two grades, as we show in the following table:

4.2.1 - Descriptive table of the Italian administrative system of *one law one jurisdictio*

FIRST GRADE	SECOND GRADE
- It is exercised by 29 (twenty-nine) Regional Administrative Courts (R.A.C.), courts of first instance spread over specific regions throughout Italy, as in the case of Lazio, whose capital is Rome, where stays one of the R.A.C. - Example of R.A.C. is given in the bidding contracts celebrated between Public Administration and third person contractors.	- It is exercised by the Council of the Presidency of the Administrative Magistracy(Consiglio di Presidenza della Magistratura Amministrativa) or Council of State. - The Council of State is provided for in art. 100 of the Italian Constitution of 1948 with dual function, in the following terms: "Il Consiglio di Stato e` organo di consulenza giuridico-amministrativa e di tutela della giustizia nell'amministrazione." Therefore, it exercises the advisory capacity of the Public Administration and of judicial protection, through its administrative judges.

Having made this brief comparison between the Brazilian and Italian administrative justice system, it follows a table with some advantages and disadvantages of the Italian system, similar to what we present about Brazilian administrative justice.

4.2.2 - Advantages and disadvantages of the Italian Administrative system of *one law one jurisdictio*

Advantages of the Italian system	Disadvantages of the Italian system
- Greater degree of specialization of those who work with administrative law. - Creation of uniform administrative jurisprudence as a means of efficiency in the provision of public services. - Decrease in the workload of the Judiciary insofar exists a specialized justice for the guarantee of administrative jurisdictional protection.	- Greater spending of public money with the maintenance of administrative Courts. - The short decadential term of impugning of the administrative acts before the Public Administration. In general, the deadline period is 60 days unlike the Brazilian term that is 5 (five) years.

CHAPTER 5

Crimes Against The Public Administrations of Mercosur and of The World Should Be Raised to The Category of Crimes Against Humanity

The Geneva International Committee is a good source for explaining crimes against humanity and the competence of the International Criminal Court to try them.

For this reason we transcribe some excerpts that demonstrate the feasibility of our proposal of raise crimes against the Public Administrations of Mercosur and of the World should be raised to the category of crimes against humanity:

"Since the end of World War II, the United Nations has repeatedly considered the idea of establishing a permanent international criminal court. In 1993 and 1994, two special tribunals were set up to punish serious violations of international humanitarian law in former Yugoslavia and in Rwanda respectively. In 1994 it began a series of negotiations to establish a permanent international criminal court with jurisdiction over the most serious crimes for the international community, regardless of where they were committed.

These negotiations culminated in the adoption in Rome of the Statute of the International Criminal Court (ICC) in July 1998, which demonstrates the decision of the international community of caring for the perpetrators of these grave crimes not without punishment. The Statute entered into force after the ratification of 60 States.

Jurisdiction of the Court

• War crimes

According to Article 8 of the Statute, the ICC has jurisdiction over war crimes, which includes most of the serious violations of international humanitarian law referred to in the Geneva Conventions and their 1977 Additional Protocols, committed both in international and non-international armed conflicts.

In the Statute several infractions were defined as war crimes, for example:

- Acts of sexual assault, sexual slavery, forced prostitution, forced pregnancy, forced sterilization or any other form of sexual violence;

- The use of children under the age of 15 to take an active part in hostilities.

The Statute does not explicitly mention any serious violations of international humanitarian law, such as unjustifiable delay in repatriation of prisoners of war and indiscriminate attacks on the civilian population or property, which are defined as grave breaches of the Geneva Conventions of 1949 or to its Additional Protocol I of 1977.

Few provisions refer to weapons whose use is prohibited by existing treaties and, in this respect, nothing is foreseen for non-international armed conflicts.

- Genocide

The ICC has jurisdiction to try the crime of genocide under Article 6 of the Statute, which reiterates the provisions of the 1948 Convention for the Prevention and Suppression of the Crime of Genocide.

This offense is covered by the Statute by any of the acts listed below, committed with intent to destroy, in whole or in part, a national, ethnic, racial or religious group as such:

- Homicide of group members;

- Serious offenses to the physical or mental integrity of members of the group;

- Intentional subjection of the group to living conditions with a view to their total or partial physical destruction;

- Imposition of measures to prevent births within the group;

- Forcibly transferring children from the group to another group.

- Crimes against humanity

The ICC can also exercise its jurisdiction over crimes against humanity. According to Article 7 of the Statute, such crimes include any of the following acts, when committed in the context of a general or systematic attack on any civilian population, with knowledge of such an attack:

- Homicide;

- Extermination;

- Slavery;

- Deportation or forced transfer of a population;

- Imprisonment or other serious deprivation of physical liberty, in violation of fundamental rules of international law;

- Torture;

- Sexual assault, sexual slavery, forced prostitution, forced pregnancy, forced sterilization or any other form of sexual violence of comparable gravity;

- Persecution of a group or collectivity that can be identified, for political, racial, national, ethnic, cultural, religious or gender-based, or other criteria universally recognized as unacceptable in international law, relating to any act referred to in this paragraph or to any crime within the jurisdiction of the Court;

- Forced disappearance of persons;

- Crime of apartheid;

- Other inhuman acts of a similar character, which intentionally cause great suffering, or seriously affect physical integrity or physical or mental health.

- Aggression

As indicated in paragraph 2 of article 5 of the Statute, the ICC may exercise its jurisdiction over the crime of aggression when a provision is approved that establishes this crime and sets forth the conditions for exercising that jurisdiction.

When can the ICC exercise its jurisdiction?

When a State becomes a Party to the Statute, it accepts the jurisdiction of the ICC on the crimes mentioned above. In accordance with Article 25 of the Statute, the Court shall exercise its jurisdiction over individuals, not States.

The ICC may exercise its jurisdiction by provocation of the Prosecutor or of a State Party, provided that one of the following Statutes is bound by the Statute:

The State in whose territory the conduct in question has taken place or, where the offense has been committed on board a ship or aircraft, the State of registry of the ship or aircraft;

State that the person to whom a crime is charged is a national.

A State which is not a party to the Statute may make a declaration accepting the jurisdiction of the Court.

Under the collective security system described in Chapter VII of the Charter of the United Nations, the Security Council may submit cases to the Prosecutor for the purpose of initiating the investigation; it may also request that no criminal investigation or prosecution be initiated or continued for a renewable period of twelve months.

Article 124 of the Rome Statute limits the possibility of exercising the jurisdiction of the ICC on war crimes. According to that provision, a

State may declare that, for a period of seven years, it will not accept the jurisdiction of the Court for war crimes presumably committed by its nationals in its territory.

National repression systems and the ICC

Under the Geneva Conventions of 1949 and Additional Protocol I of 1977, States must bring before the domestic courts those accused of committing war crimes or extraditing them for trial in another country. Nothing in the Statute exempts States from their obligations under customary instruments or rules of international humanitarian law.

Under the principle of complementarity, the jurisdiction of the ICC should be exercised only where a State cannot or does not wish to prosecute alleged war criminals under its jurisdiction. In order to benefit from this principle, however, States need adequate legislation to enable them to prosecute such criminals.

In addition, States parties to international humanitarian law treaties should enact rules for the implementation of these treaties in order to give effect to the obligations assumed in ratifying such instruments.

What is needed to secure the ICCs jurisdiction?

- States should ratify the TPI Statute as soon as possible, since universal ratification is essential for the Court to be able to exercise its jurisdiction and forcefully and whenever necessary;

- States should refrain from using the exception clause (Article 124 of the Statute);

- States should thoroughly examine their national legislation to ensure that they can avail themselves of the principle of complementarity, on which the ICC is founded, and to judge individuals for breaches of the Court's jurisdiction in accordance with their own legal systems;

- States should cooperate with each other and with the ICC regarding trials of crimes within the jurisdiction of the Court. By doing so, they will have to enact appropriate laws or modify their legislation, including the delivery of persons accused of such crimes.

Towards an integral system of repression

National courts will continue to play an important and primary role in prosecuting alleged war crimes. In addition, the establishment of the ICC does not in any way impede the work undertaken by the aforementioned special tribunals (for former Yugoslavia and Rwanda), which were instituted to punish crimes related to specific situations (the first, for crimes committed in the former Yugoslavia since 1991 and the second for those committed in Rwanda or by Rwandan citizens in neighboring countries in 1994).

The establishment of the International Criminal Court is a further step towards effective repression of those responsible for the world's most serious crimes. States are urged to ratify the Statute of the Court so that they cease to enjoy impunity." (see it in http://www.icrc.org/por/resources/documents/misc/5yblr2.htm. Acess in 15.02.2014)

Rui Carlos Dissenha, Master of Social Relations Law at the Federal University of Paraná, addressed the theme of crimes against humanity, its concept and its negative effects for the community of nations so as to leave no doubt that the criminalization of crimes against humanity goes to meet the objectives of law by demonstrating that they translate for certainty that humanity has protection against the state when it tramples on its rights in an outrageous way to the conscience of humanity.

Here is an excerpt from what he says:

"2.2. The Second World War and crimes against humanity:

Unlike the above scenarios, in World War II the Allies became aware of the gravity of the situation and understood that a clear and precise definition of the concept was essential. Otherwise, the heinous acts practiced by the Axis powers during and before the conflict would be lost in history. After all, up to that time, for example, nothing in International Customs Law has classified as a crime, in an obvious way, acts like the persecution for political or racial reasons of nationals of some State. The most similar crime, admitted by the Law of War of that time, was that of persecution of enemies, which evidently did not involve nationals of the State itself. In this way, therefore, the example of Nazi persecution of ethnic minorities did not fit into any criminal definition since they were German citizens. Thus, the command of the Allied forces decided to materialize crimes against humanity within the statutes of the military courts created for the judgment of the Axis powers. Although imperfect and tainted as courts created by the victors to judge the vanquished, the military courts of Nuremberg and Tokyo represent a forceful development of International Criminal Law.

Thus, it is undisputed that the first effective declaration on crimes against humanity was made in the Statute of the Court of Nuremberg, in article 6, c'11. Then, the Statute of the Court of Tokyo also defined and in a very similar way, the crime against humanity in article 5, c'12.

According to CASSESE, the issues raised by the Military Courts of Nuremberg and Tokyo, although imperfect and applied in an "ad hoc" and "post factum" situation, are of extreme importance for two specific reasons: "first, it states that the international community was broadening the category of acts considered to be of 'meta-national' interest (...) Secondly, in as much as crimes against humanity were punishable even when committed without breaking national law, the 1945 Agreement showed that in some special circumstances there are limits to the omnipotence of the State (...) and that the ultimate goal of all law is not disregarded for the protection of humanity when the State tramples on its rights in an outrageous way to the conscience of humanity."

I had the opportunity to attend a lecture by Professor Mireille Delmas-Marty at the World Congress of Criminology in Barra da Tijuca, Rio de Janeiro, in 2004 on the challenges of creating a world right that better protects the rights of humanity.

In his book "Three Challenges for a World Right. Translation and afterword of Fauzi Hassan Choukr. Rio de Janeiro: Lumen Juris, 2003. p. 183-184, "Delmas-Marty says:

"In the Nuremberg Tribunal's statute, the concept of crime against humanity did indeed cease to evolve, by a kind of curious relation between the rule of law, at the height of its coldness, and events throughout its horror, no doubt. In Nuremberg, crimes against humanity are nests after crimes against peace and war crimes such as: "Murder slavery, deportation and any other inhuman act committed against any civilian population, before or during the war, or persecution for racial or religious political reasons "(Article 6). of the Statute of the Court, 1945). In the later texts of the UN and the Council of Europe, the imprescriptibility (Conventions of November 1968 and January 25, 1948) is added to the reference to genocide such as that of the UN Convention in 1948 The mention of the inhuman acts resulting from the Apharteid's policy, the crime of Apharteid, was itself included in the Convention of November 1973.

The next stage will be the creation of international criminal courts: initially, the so-called ad hoc tribunals, this term already mentioned marking the boundaries in space (for former Yugoslavia and Rwanda) and in time (duration of the armed conflict) within the jurisdiction of those jurisdictions. Prepared by various committees of international experts, in particular by the French committee chaired by Pierre Truche, then by a first UN Security Council resolution, by a substantial report of the Secretary-General of the UN, the Hague Tribunal will have been finally put into operation by the well-known resolution 827 (May 25, 1993). Then the Aruhah, created by the resolution of 8 November 1994 for Rwanda, proclaimed on 3 January 1994 the first condemnation for genocide against the former Prime Minister responsible for the extermination of some 800,000 Tutsis between April and July 1994.

Professor Mireille (2003: 183-187-188), analyzing in a masterly way the thinking of Hanna Arendt on the plural conception of humankind, afirms that:

> "An impossible task," said Hanna Arendt, "but she gave the key by insisting on the need for a plural conception of humanity: it is not the man who inhabits the earth, it is men.

> It is, in fact, a plural conception that always pervades the list of crimes against humanity. If there is always, as we have seen, a collective basis for these prohibitions, the humanity that comprises these crimes is not a totalitarian humanity. The prohibition means that a human being, even deeply embedded in his family, cultural or religious community, must never lose his individuality and be reduced to a mere element that can be changed by others and rejected as such (to kill someone not for what he but because he was born, said André Frossard, it is the crime against humanity. If the human being needs to belong to a group, he cannot be locked, caged, in his direction without losing his status to humanity. In short, what if the rma is the singularity of each human being and its equal belonging to the human community. This implies that crimes against humanity are not confined to the destruction of human beings, it can encompass deliberate political, legal, medical or scientific practices that seemingly respect life, but they check humanity as understood. In addition to the survival of the species, it is the conception of human dignity that is at stake here with the definition of these crimes, which should in turn include any violation of the principle of singularity (exclusion, even exterminating human groups reduced to a racial, ethnic, genetic category, notably by cloning) and that of equal membership of a human community (discriminatory practices such as apartheid, or the creation of "supermen" by genetic selection or "sub-men" by the growth of the species, becoming eugenics a simple variation).

It is a fact that today's world needs much more than a proliferation of ideologically worked rules to pass on a sense of the amount of state judicial protection.

The anarchy that was formerly known by the absence of order or laws, today appears as the fruit of the excess of useless laws, impossible to be fulfilled laws, ineffective and tending to the preservation of impunity laws.

It is irreproachable the thoughts of Mireille Delmas-Marty (2003: 19-20), in his approach to the paradox between the universal rights of man and his individual universe:

> "The universality of human rights refers primarily to a mental universe rather than to a real universe. Endorsed by the Universal Declaration of 1948, it is essentially still to be built. It is, therefore, like the economic globalization of an ongoing process that has the questions raised by its apparent fragility. However, this process, which can be said of 'universalization', does not lead to the diffusion of a single model, starting from a single point, but above all to emergence, in several points of the same desire to recognize the rights common to all human beings. In this sense, universality implies more a sharing of meanings and even an enrichment of meanings by the exchange between cultures: "In fact, all societies live something of the requirements of human rights, but each in its own way ". It is then a question of bringing these "different ways" together so that they interpenetrate and enrich each other. More than a single way, the uni¬ versal Declaration opens up innumerable paths of crossing, sometimes without direction, like some of the routes that are part of the first primates until Homo Sapiens. But hominality has taken millennia and is undoubtedly unfinished, as witnessed precisely by the debate on the universality of human rights."

It is time to acknowledge that isolated and systemic acts of corruption that deflect trillions of dollars a year around the world mercilessly kill more than Islamic terrorism, African tribal wars and conflicts, and other forms of genocide throughout the world.

We can discuss genocides and genocidas on all continents, but none of them is as cruel as the politician and public officials, authors of the deviation of public money that kills millions of people in the corridors of public hospitals, ind the streets and by hungry every day around the world.

We need urgently more Ethics and less hypocrisy, which is the practice of claiming to have moral standards or beliefs to which one's own behavior does not conform. We see it in every state of rule, in every politician speach and in the daily life of peoples as the result of the decadence of the educational process of the societies.

No genocide has ever killed as many people as hungry does in Africa, Latin America and parts of Asia, while their own governments swims in pools of money

If true the statements of the world media, which say that 28 thousand people die of hunger every day, that number by 365 days represents more than 10 millions dies of hunger a year.

There is no doubt that most of these deaths occur because the public policies of our democratic states of rule are not implemented because of politicians and public officials who routinely loot public treasury by isolated and systemic acts of corruption.

The Universal Declaration of Human Rights is assertive to saying that we are worthy of the substantial tutelage of the all Articles XXII to XVIII are expressed as to such rights. Let's see:

"Article XXII

Every person, as a member of society, has the right to social security and to the realization, by national effort, international cooperation, and in accordance with the organization and resources of each State, of the indispensable economic, social and cultural rights his dignity and the free development of his personality.

Article XXIII

1. Everyone has the right to work, to free choice of employment, to just and favorable conditions of work and to protection against unemployment.

2. Every person, without any distinction, is entitled to equal remuneration for equal work.

3. Every person who is employed shall have the right to a fair and satisfactory remuneration which guarantees him and his family an existence compatible with human dignity and to which other means of protection shall be added where necessary Social.

4. Everyone has the right to form and to join trade unions for the protection of his interests.

Article XXIV

Everyone has the right to rest and leisure, including reasonable limitation of working hours and periodic holidays with pay.

Article XXV

1. Everyone has the right to a standard of living adequate for him and his family's health and well-being, including food, clothing, housing, medical care and essential social services, and the right to security in case of unemployment, illness, invalidity, widowhood, old age or other cases of loss of means of subsistence beyond his control.

2. Maternity and childhood have the right to special care and assistance. All children born in or out of wedlock will enjoy the same social protection.

Article XXVI

1. Everyone has the right to education. The instruction will be free, at least in elementary and fundamental degrees. Elementary education shall be compulsory. The technical-proffesional instruction will be accessible to all, as well as the higher education, it is based on merit.

2. The instruction shall be directed towards the full development of the human personality and the strengthening of respect for human rights and fundamental freedoms. Education will promote understanding, tolerance and friendship among all nations and racial or religious groups, and will support United Nations peace-keeping activities.

3. Parents have a prior right to choose the kind of instruction that will be given to their children.

Article XXVII

1. Everyone has the right freely to participate in the cultural life of the community, to enjoy the arts and to participate in the scientific process and its benefits.

2. Everyone has the right to the protection of the moral and material interests resulting from any scientific, literary or artistic production of which he is the author.

Article XVIII

Everyone has the right to a social and international order in which the rights and freedoms set forth in this Declaration can be fully realized."

The Mercosur constitutions formally reiterate that everyone has a social and international order in which the established rights and freedoms are preserved, but corruption with public monies has clearly prevented such results.

Two actions can change the course of this story:

1) That the people learn to exercise their free right of resistance against corrupt governments; and

2) That corrupt politician or public official be identified and punished in an exemplary way, so that the new generations are educated to love the republic and the people.

We urgently need to criminalize acts of corruption with public money as a crime against humanity, because to divert public money is an action that kills purposefully, it is genocide commited daily by by politicians with guns with mufflers attached. The guns of the political powers.

FINAL CONSIDERATIONS ON BOOK IV

It is important to note that in many cases what constitutes an advantage for the State Administration may be a disadvantage for the public service user, as administrative instances in which the Brazilian public advocacy is forced to postpone judicial performance to the maximum extent, due to the lack of sufficient functional independence to allow decisions that are more in line with the Justice, than in accordance with the law.

We believe that the creation in Brazil of one more Special Administrative Justice, such as labor, electoral and military, fulfills the constitutional purpose, principally in art. 37 of the 1988 Constitution, when it cries out for the efficience in the provision of public services.

A specialized administrative magistracy would provide more speed, income and adequacy in the protection of clients-citizens rights.

The Brazilian Federal Constitution has politically and legally structured its Public Administration, but at no time has it created an administrative system with administrative judges and Courts, as did Italy with its Regional Administrative Courts and with the State Council.

International Law may combine the best of the logical-dialectical process, as it proceeds to investigate and propose solutions to produce the necessary "universal" synthesis between the theses and antitheses of national legal systems.

The legislative instruments of the International Law, such as the Inter-American Convention Against Corruption (IACAC) and the Convention against Corruption (UNCAC), among others, can help in the fight against misery and the creation of real substantial democracies. Don't we need them?

ANNEX I

Inter-American Convention Against Corruption (IACAC)

DECREE No. 4,410, OF OCTOBER 7, 2002.

It promulgates the Inter-American Convention against Corruption, of March 29, 1996, subject to art. XI, paragraph 1, subsection "c".

THE PRESIDENT OF THE REPUBLIC, in the use of the attribution conferred by art. 84, subsection VIII, of the Constitution,

Considering that the National Congress approved, through Legislative Decree 152 of June 25, 2002, the text of the Inter-American Convention against Corruption, adopted in Caracas on March 29, 1996, subject to art. XI, paragraph 1, subsection "c";

Considering that the Convention entered into force for Brazil on August 24, 2002, in accordance with its Article XXV;

DECREES:

Art. 1 The Inter-American Convention against Corruption, adopted in Caracas on March 29, 1996, appended by a copy of this Decree, shall be executed and fulfilled as fully as it is contained therein, subject to art. XI, paragraph 1, subsection "c". (Redaction given by Decree No. 4,534, dated 12.19.2002)

Art. 2 Any acts that may result in a revision of the aforementioned Convention, as well as any complementary terms of art. 49, item I, of the Constitution, entail burdensome commitments or commitments to the national patrimony.

Article 3 This Decree shall enter into force on the date of its publication.

Brasília, October 7, 2002; 181st of Independence and 114th of Republic.

FERNANDO HENRIQUE CARDOSO Celso Lafer

This text does not replace the one published in D.O.U. of 8.10.2002

INTER-AMERICAN CONVENTION AGAINST CORPORATION

Adopted at the third plenary session, held on March 29, 1996)

PREAMBLE

THE MEMBER STATES OF THE ORGANIZATION OF AMERICAN STATES,

CONVINCED that corruption undermines the legitimacy of public institutions and strikes at society, moral order and justice, as well as at the comprehensive development of peoples;

CONSIDERING that representative democracy, an essential condition for stability, peace and development of the region, requires, by its nature, the combating of every form of corruption in the performance of public functions, as well as acts of corruption specifically related to such performance;

PERSUADED that fighting corruption strengthens democratic institutions and prevents distortions in the economy, improprieties in public administration and damage to a society's moral fiber;

RECOGNIZING that corruption is often a tool used by organized crime for the accomplishment of its purposes;

CONVINCED of the importance of making people in the countries of the region aware of this problem and its gravity, and of the need to strengthen participation by civil society in preventing and fighting corruption;

RECOGNIZING that, in some cases, corruption has international dimensions, which requires coordinated action by States to fight it effectively;

CONVINCED of the need for prompt adoption of an international instrument to promote and facilitate international cooperation in fighting corruption and, especially, in taking appropriate action against persons who commit acts of corruption in the performance of public functions, or acts specifically related to such performance, as well as appropriate measures with respect to the proceeds of such acts;

DEEPLY CONCERNED by the steadily increasing links between corruption and the proceeds generated by illicit narcotics trafficking which undermine and threaten legitimate commercial and financial activities, and society, at all levels;

BEARING IN MIND the responsibility of States to hold corrupt persons accountable in order to combat corruption and to cooperate with one another for their efforts in this area to be effective; and

DETERMINED to make every effort to prevent, detect, punish and eradicate corruption in the performance of public functions and acts of corruption specifically related to such performance,

HAVE AGREED

to adopt the following

INTER-AMERICAN CONVENTION AGAINST CORRUPTION

Article I
Definitions

For the purposes of this Convention:

"Public function" means any temporary or permanent, paid or honorary activity, performed by a natural person in the name of the State or in the service of the State or its institutions, at any level of its hierarchy.

"Public official", "government official", or "public servant" means any official or employee of the State or its agencies, including those who have been selected, appointed, or elected to perform activities or functions in the name of the State or in the service of the State, at any level of its hierarchy.

"Property" means assets of any kind, whether movable or immovable, tangible or intangible, and any document or legal instrument demonstrating, purporting to demonstrate, or relating to ownership or other rights pertaining to such assets.

Article II
Purposes

The purposes of this Convention are:

1. To promote and strengthen the development by each of the States Parties of the mechanisms needed to prevent, detect, punish and eradicate corruption; and

2. To promote, facilitate and regulate cooperation among the States Parties to ensure the effectiveness of measures and actions to prevent, detect, punish and eradicate corruption in the performance of public functions and acts of corruption specifically related to such performance.

Article III
Preventive Measures

For the purposes set forth in Article II of this Convention, the States Parties agree to consider the applicability of measures within their own institutional systems to create, maintain and strengthen:

1. Standards of conduct for the correct, honorable, and proper fulfillment of public functions. These standards shall be intended to prevent conflicts of interest and mandate the proper conservation and use of resources entrusted to government officials in the performance of their functions. These standards shall also establish measures and systems requiring government officials to report to appropriate authorities acts of corruption in the performance of public functions. Such measures should help preserve the public's confidence in the integrity of public servants and government processes.

2. Mechanisms to enforce these standards of conduct.

3. Instruction to government personnel to ensure proper understanding of their responsibilities and the ethical rules governing their activities.

4. Systems for registering the income, assets and liabilities of persons who perform public functions in certain posts as specified by law and, where appropriate, for making such registrations public.

5. Systems of government hiring and procurement of goods and services that assure the openness, equity and efficiency of such systems.

6. Government revenue collection and control systems that deter corruption.

7. Laws that deny favorable tax treatment for any individual or corporation for expenditures made in violation of the anticorruption laws of the States Parties.

8. Systems for protecting public servants and private citizens who, in good faith, report acts of corruption, including protection of their identities,

in accordance with their Constitutions and the basic principles of their domestic legal systems.

9. Oversight bodies with a view to implementing modern mechanisms for preventing, detecting, punishing and eradicating corrupt acts.

10. Deterrents to the bribery of domestic and foreign government officials, such as mechanisms to ensure that publicly held companies and other types of associations maintain books and records which, in reasonable detail, accurately reflect the acquisition and disposition of assets, and have sufficient internal accounting controls to enable their officers to detect corrupt acts.

11. Mechanisms to encourage participation by civil society and nongovernmental organizations in efforts to prevent corruption.

12. The study of further preventive measures that take into account the relationship between equitable compensation and probity in public service. Article IV Scope This Convention is applicable provided that the alleged act of corruption has been committed or has effects in a State Party.

Article V
Jurisdiction

1. Each State Party shall adopt such measures as may be necessary to establish its jurisdiction over the offenses it has established in accordance with this Convention when the offense in question is committed in its territory.

2. Each State Party may adopt such measures as may be necessary to establish its jurisdiction over the offenses it has established in accordance with this Convention when the offense is committed by one of its nationals or by a person who habitually resides in its territory.

3. Each State Party shall adopt such measures as may be necessary to establish its jurisdiction over the offenses it has established in accordance with this Convention when the alleged criminal is present in its territory

and it does not extradite such person to another country on the ground of the nationality of the alleged criminal.

4. This Convention does not preclude the application of any other rule of criminal jurisdiction established by a State Party under its domestic law.

Article VI
Acts of Corruption

1. This Convention is applicable to the following acts of corruption:

a. The solicitation or acceptance, directly or indirectly, by a government official or a person who performs public functions, of any article of monetary value, or other benefit, such as a gift, favor, promise or advantage for himself or for another person or entity, in exchange for any act or omission in the performance of his public functions;

b. The offering or granting, directly or indirectly, to a government official or a person who performs public functions, of any article of monetary value, or other benefit, such as a gift, favor, promise or advantage for himself or for another person or entity, in exchange for any act or omission in the performance of his public functions;

c. Any act or omission in the discharge of his duties by a government official or a person who performs public functions for the purpose of illicitly obtaining benefits for himself or for a third party;

d. The fraudulent use or concealment of property derived from any of the acts referred to in this article; and

e. Participation as a principal, coprincipal, instigator, accomplice or accessory after the fact, or in any other manner, in the commission or attempted commission of, or in any collaboration or conspiracy to commit, any of the acts referred to in this article.

2. This Convention shall also be applicable by mutual agreement between or among two or more States Parties with respect to any other act of corruption not described herein.

Article VII
Domestic Law

The States Parties that have not yet done so shall adopt the necessary legislative or other measures to establish as criminal offenses under their domestic law the acts of corruption described in Article VI(1) and to facilitate cooperation among themselves pursuant to this Convention.

Article VIII
Transnational Bribery

Subject to its Constitution and the fundamental principles of its legal system, each State Party shall prohibit and punish the offering or granting, directly or indirectly, by its nationals, persons having their habitual residence in its territory, and businesses domiciled there, to a government official of another State, of any article of monetary value, or other benefit, such as a gift, favor, promise or advantage, in connection with any economic or commercial transaction in exchange for any act or omission in the performance of that official's public functions.

Among those States Parties that have established transnational bribery as an offense, such offense shall be considered an act of corruption for the purposes of this Convention.

Any State Party that has not established transnational bribery as an offense shall, insofar as its laws permit, provide assistance and cooperation with respect to this offense as provided in this Convention.

Article IX
Illicit Enrichment

Subject to its Constitution and the fundamental principles of its legal system, each State Party that has not yet done so shall take the necessary measures to establish under its laws as an offense a significant increase in the assets of a government official that he cannot reasonably explain in relation to his lawful earnings during the performance of his functions.

Among those States Parties that have established illicit enrichment as an offense, such offense shall be considered an act of corruption for the purposes of this Convention.

Any State Party that has not established illicit enrichment as an offense shall, insofar as its laws permit, provide assistance and cooperation with respect to this offense as provided in this Convention.

Article X
Notification

When a State Party adopts the legislation referred to in paragraph 1 of articles VIII and IX, it shall notify the Secretary General of the Organization of American States, who shall in turn notify the other States Parties. For the purposes of this Convention, the crimes of transnational bribery and illicit enrichment shall be considered acts of corruption for that State Party thirty days following the date of such notification.

Article XI
Progressive Development

1. In order to foster the development and harmonization of their domestic legislation and the attainment of the purposes of this Convention, the States Parties view as desirable, and undertake to consider, establishing as offenses under their laws the following acts:

a. The improper use by a government official or a person who performs public functions, for his own benefit or that of a third party, of any kind of classified or confidential information which that official or person who performs public functions has obtained because of, or in the performance of, his functions;

b. The improper use by a government official or a person who performs public functions, for his own benefit or that of a third party, of any kind of property belonging to the State or to any firm or institution in which the State has a proprietary interest, to which that official or person who performs public functions has access because of, or in the performance of, his functions;

c. Any act or omission by any person who, personally or through a third party, or acting as an intermediary, seeks to obtain a decision from a public authority whereby he illicitly obtains for himself or for another person any benefit or gain, whether or not such act or omission harms State property; and

d. The diversion by a government official, for purposes unrelated to those for which they were intended, for his own benefit or that of a third party, of any movable or immovable property, monies or securities belonging to the State, to an independent agency, or to an individual, that such official has received by virtue of his position for purposes of administration, custody or for other reasons.

2. Among those States Parties that have established these offenses, such offenses shall be considered acts of corruption for the purposes of this Convention.

3. Any State Party that has not established these offenses shall, insofar as its laws permit, provide assistance and cooperation with respect to these offenses as provided in this Convention.

Article XII
Effect on State Property

For application of this Convention, it shall not be necessary that the acts of corruption harm State property.

Article XIII
Extradition

1. This article shall apply to the offenses established by the States Parties in accordance with this Convention.

2. Each of the offenses to which this article applies shall be deemed to be included as an extraditable offense in any extradition treaty existing between or among the States Parties. The States Parties undertake to include such offenses as extraditable offenses in every extradition treaty to be concluded between or among them.

3. If a State Party that makes extradition conditional on the existence of a treaty receives a request for extradition from another State Party with which it does not have an extradition treaty, it may consider this Convention as the legal basis for extradition with respect to any offense to which this article applies.

4. States Parties that do not make extradition conditional on the existence of a treaty shall recognize offenses to which this article applies as extraditable offenses between themselves.

5. Extradition shall be subject to the conditions provided for by the law of the Requested State or by applicable extradition treaties, including the grounds on which the Requested State may refuse extradition.

6. If extradition for an offense to which this article applies is refused solely on the basis of the nationality of the person sought, or because the Requested State deems that it has jurisdiction over the offense, the Requested State shall submit the case to its competent authorities for the purpose of prosecution unless otherwise agreed with the Requesting State, and shall report the final outcome to the Requesting State in due course.

7. Subject to the provisions of its domestic law and its extradition treaties, the Requested State may, upon being satisfied that the circumstances so warrant and are urgent, and at the request of the Requesting State, take into custody a person whose extradition is sought and who is present in its territory, or take other appropriate measures to ensure his presence at extradition proceedings.

Article XIV
Assistance and Cooperation

1. In accordance with their domestic laws and applicable treaties, the States Parties shall afford one another the widest measure of mutual assistance by processing requests from authorities that, in conformity with their domestic laws, have the power to investigate or prosecute the acts of corruption described in this Convention, to obtain evidence and take other necessary action to facilitate legal proceedings and measures regarding the investigation or prosecution of acts of corruption.

2. The States Parties shall also provide each other with the widest measure of mutual technical cooperation on the most effective ways and means of preventing, detecting, investigating and punishing acts of corruption. To that end, they shall foster exchanges of experiences by way of agreements and meetings between competent bodies and institutions, and shall pay special attention to methods and procedures of citizen participation in the fight against corruption.

Article XV
Measures Regarding Property

1. In accordance with their applicable domestic laws and relevant treaties or other agreements that may be in force between or among them, the States Parties shall provide each other the broadest possible measure of assistance in the identification, tracing, freezing, seizure and forfeiture of property or proceeds obtained, derived from or used in the commission of offenses established in accordance with this Convention.

2. A State Party that enforces its own or another State Party's forfeiture judgment against property or proceeds described in paragraph 1 of this article shall dispose of the property or proceeds in accordance with its laws. To the extent permitted by a State Party's laws and upon such terms as it deems appropriate, it may transfer all or part of such property or proceeds to another State Party that assisted in the underlying investigation or proceedings.

Article XVI
Bank Secrecy

1. The Requested State shall not invoke bank secrecy as a basis for refusal to provide the assistance sought by the Requesting State. The Requested State shall apply this article in accordance with its domestic law, its procedural provisions, or bilateral or multilateral agreements with the Requesting State.

2. The Requesting State shall be obligated not to use any information received that is protected by bank secrecy for any purpose other than the

proceeding for which that information was requested, unless authorized by the Requested State.

Article XVII
Nature of the Act

For the purposes of articles XIII, XIV, XV and XVI of this Convention, the fact that the property obtained or derived from an act of corruption was intended for political purposes, or that it is alleged that an act of corruption was committed for political motives or purposes, shall not suffice in and of itself to qualify the act as a political offense or as a common offense related to a political offense.

Article XVIII
Central Authorities

1. For the purposes of international assistance and cooperation provided under this Convention, each State Party may designate a central authority or may rely upon such central authorities as are provided for in any relevant treaties or other agreements.

2. The central authorities shall be responsible for making and receiving the requests for assistance and cooperation referred to in this Convention.

3. The central authorities shall communicate with each other directly for the purposes of this Convention.

Article XIX
Temporal Application

Subject to the constitutional principles and the domestic laws of each State and existing treaties between the States Parties, the fact that the alleged act of corruption was committed before this Convention entered into force shall not preclude procedural cooperation in criminal matters between the States Parties. This provision shall in no case affect the principle of non-retroactivity in criminal law, nor shall application of this provision interrupt existing statutes of limitations relating to crimes committed prior to the date of the entry into force of this Convention.

Article XX
Other Agreements or Practices

No provision of this Convention shall be construed as preventing the States Parties from engaging in mutual cooperation within the framework of other international agreements, bilateral or multilateral, currently in force or concluded in the future, or pursuant to any other applicable arrangement or practice.

Article XXI
Signature

This Convention is open for signature by the Member States of the Organization of American States.

Article XXII
Ratification

This Convention is subject to ratification. The instruments of ratification shall be deposited with the General Secretariat of the Organization of American States.

Article XXIII
Accession

This Convention shall remain open for accession by any other State. The instruments of accession shall be deposited with the General Secretariat of the Organization of American States.

Article XXIV
Reservations

The States Parties may, at the time of adoption, signature, ratification, or accession, make reservations to this Convention, provided that each reservation concerns one or more specific provisions and is not incompatible with the object and purpose of the Convention.

Article XXV
Entry Into Force

This Convention shall enter into force on the thirtieth day following the date of deposit of the second instrument of ratification. For each State ratifying or acceding to the Convention after the deposit of the second instrument of ratification, the Convention shall enter into force on the thirtieth day after deposit by such State of its instrument of ratification or accession.

Article XXVI
Denunciation

This Convention shall remain in force indefinitely, but any of the States Parties may denounce it. The instrument of denunciation shall be deposited with the General Secretariat of the Organization of American States. One year from the date of deposit of the instrument of denunciation, the Convention shall cease to be in force for the denouncing State, but shall remain in force for the other States Parties.

Article XXVII
Additional Protocols

Any State Party may submit for the consideration of other States Parties meeting at a General Assembly of the Organization of American States draft additional protocols to this Convention to contribute to the attainment of the purposes set forth in Article II thereof. Each additional protocol shall establish the terms for its entry into force and shall apply only to those States that become Parties to it.

Article XXVIII
Deposit of Original Instrument

The original instrument of this Convention, the English, French, Portuguese, and Spanish texts of which are equally authentic, shall be deposited with the General Secretariat of the Organization of American States, which shall forward an authenticated copy of its text to the Secretariat of the United Nations for registration and publication in accordance with Article 102 of the United Nations Charter. The General Secretariat of the Organization of American States shall notify its Member States and the States that have acceded to the Convention of signatures, of the deposit of instruments of ratification, accession, or denunciation, and of reservations, if any.

ANNEX II

United Nations Convention against Corruption — UNCAC

DECREE No. 5.687, OF JANUARY 31, 2006.

It promulgates the United Nations Convention against Corruption, adopted by the General Assembly of the United Nations on October 31, 2003 and signed by Brazil on December 9, 2003.

THE PRESIDENT OF THE REPUBLIC, in the use of the attribution conferred by art. 84, section IV, of the Constitution, and

Considering that the National Congress approved the text of the United Nations Convention against Corruption, through Legislative Decree 348 of May 18, 2005;

Whereas the Brazilian Government ratified the said Convention on June 15, 2005;

Considering that the Convention entered into force internationally, as well as for Brazil, on December 14, 2005;

DECREES:

Article 1 The United Nations Convention against Corruption, adopted by the General Assembly of the United Nations on October 31, 2003, and signed by Brazil on December 9, 2003, appended by a copy of this Decree, shall be executed and complied with as fully contained in it.

Art. 2 Any acts that may result in a revision of the said Convention or which entail burdensome charges or commitments to the national patrimony, shall be subject to the approval of the National Congress, pursuant to art. 49, item I, of the Constitution.

Article 3 This Decree shall enter into force on the date of its publication.

Brasília, January 31, 2006; 185th of Independence and of the Republic.

LUIZ INÁCIO LULA DA SILVA Celso Luiz Nunes Amorim

This text does not replace the one published in the DOU of 01.2.2006

UNITED NATIONS CONVENTION AGAINST CORRUPTION

Preamble

The States Parties to this Convention, Concerned with the seriousness of the problems and the threats to corruption, stability and security of societies, by undermining the institutions and values of democracy, ethics and justice and by undermining sustainable development and the rule of law;

Concerned also by the links between corruption and other forms of delinquency, in particular organized crime and economic corruption, including money laundering;

Concerned also by cases of corruption that penetrate various sectors of society, which may jeopardize a significant proportion of States' resources and threaten political stability and sustainable development;

Convinced that corruption has ceased to be a local problem in order to become a transnational phenomenon affecting all societies and economies, international co-operation is needed to prevent and fight against it;

Convinced, also, that a comprehensive and multidisciplinary approach is required to prevent and combat corruption;

Convinced that the availability of technical assistance can play an important role in enabling States to combat and actively combat corruption, among other things, by strengthening their capacities and creating institutions;

Convinced that illicit personal enrichment can be particularly harmful to democratic institutions, national economies and the rule of law;

Determined to prevent, detect and deter international transfers of illicitly acquired assets more efficiently and to strengthen international cooperation for the recovery of these assets;

Recognizing the fundamental principles of due process in criminal proceedings and in civil or administrative procedures relating to property rights;

Bearing in mind that prevention and eradication of corruption are the responsibility of all States and that they should cooperate with each other, with the support and participation of persons and groups not belonging to the public sector, such as society civil society organizations, non-governmental organizations and community-based organizations, so that their efforts in this field will be effective;

Bearing in mind also the principles of proper management of public affairs and goods, equity, accountability and equality before the law, as well as the need to safeguard integrity and foster a culture of rejection of corruption;

Commending the work of the Commission on Crime Prevention and Criminal Justice and the United Nations Office on Drugs and Crime in preventing and combating corruption;

Recalling the work carried out by other international and regional organizations in this field, including the activities of the Customs Cooperation Council (also known as the World Customs Organization), the European Council, the League of Arab States, the Organization for Co-operation and Development The Organization of American States, the African Union and the European Union;

Noting with appreciation the multilateral instruments to prevent and combat corruption, including, inter alia, the Inter-American Convention against Corruption, adopted by the Organization of American States on 29 March 1996, the Convention on the Fight against Corruption involving officials of the European Communities and States Parties of the European Union, approved by the Council of the European Union on 26 May 1997, the Convention on the fight against bribery of foreign public servants in international commercial transactions, approved by the Committee of Ministers of the European Council on 27 January 1999, the Civil Law Convention on Corruption adopted by the The Committee of Ministers of the European Council on 4 November 1999 and the African Union Convention to Prevent and Combat Corruption, adopted by the Heads of State and Government of the African Union on 12 July 2003;

Welcoming the entry into force on 29 September 2003 of the United Nations Convention against Transnational Organized Crime;

Have agreed as follows:

Chapter I General provisions

Article 1 Purpose
The purpose of this Convention is to:

(a) Promote and strengthen measures to prevent and combat corruption more effectively and efficiently;

(b) Promote, facilitate and support international cooperation and technical assistance in preventing and combating corruption, including asset recovery;

c) Promote integrity, accountability and proper management of public affairs and assets.

Article 2 Definitions
For the purposes of this Convention:

(a) "civil servant" means: (I) any person holding a legislative, executive, administrative oran official of a State Party, already appointed or sworn in, permanent or temporary, paid or honorary, irrespective of the time of such person in office; (II) any person who performs a public function, including a public body or a public undertaking, or who performs a public service, which is governed by the domestic law of the State Party and which applies in the relevant sphere of that State's legal system; State Party; (III) any person appointed as a "public official" in the domestic law of a State Party. Nevertheless, for the purposes of some specific measures included in Chapter II of this Convention, "public servants" may be understood as meaning any person who performs a public function or performs a public service second in the domestic law of the State Party and applies in the relevant sphere of the legal system of that State Party;

b) "foreign public official" means any person holding a legislative, executive, administrative or judicial position of a foreign country, already appointed or sworn in; and any person performing a public function for a foreign country, including a public body or a public undertaking;

(c) "official of a public international organization" shall mean an international public official or any person that such organization has authorized to act on its behalf;

d) "assets" means assets of any kind, whether tangible or intangible, movable or immovable, tangible or intangible, and legal documents or instruments that credit the ownership or other rights to such assets;

e) "proceeds of crime" means assets of any kind derived or obtained directly or indirectly from the occurrence of a crime;

(f) "Preemptive attachment" or "seizure" shall mean a temporary prohibition on the transfer, conversion or transfer of property, or on the custody or temporary control of property on the basis of an order of a court or other competent authority ;

(g) "Con" shall mean deprivation of property, by order of a court or other competent authority;

(h) "Crimes" shall mean any offense from which a product is derived which may become the subject of a misdemeanor in Article 23 of this Convention;

(i) "Surveyed delivery" means the technique of allowing illicit or suspicious consignments to leave the territory of one or more States, to pass through or enter it, with the knowledge and under the supervision of their competent authorities, with the to investigate a crime and to identify the persons involved in its occurrence.

Article 3 Scope

1. This Convention shall apply, in accordance with its provisions, to the prevention, investigation and judicial investigation of corruption and the freezing, seizure, confiscation and restitution of proceeds of crime identified in accordance with this Convention. Convention.

2. For the purposes of this Convention, unless it contains a provision to the contrary, it shall not be necessary for the offenses set forth therein to cause the State damage or prejudice to the State.

Article 4 Protection of sovereignty

1. States Parties shall comply with their obligations under this Convention in accordance with the principles of sovereign equality and territorial integrity of States and of non-interference in the internal affairs of other States.

2. Nothing in this Convention shall delegate powers to a State Party to exercise, in the territory of another State, jurisdiction or functions which the domestic law of that State reserves exclusively to its authorities.

Chapter II
Preventive measures

Article 5
Policies and practices to prevent corruption

1. Each State Party shall, in accordance with the fundamental principles of its legal system, formulate and implement or maintain in force coordinated and anti-corruption policies that promote the participation of society and respect the principles of the rule of law, proper management of public affairs and property, integrity, transparency and accountability.

2. Each State Party shall endeavor to establish and foster practices and practices aimed at preventing corruption.

3. Each State Party shall endeavor to periodically evaluate relevant legal instruments and administrative measures to determine whether they are adequate to combat corruption.

4. States Parties, as appropriate and in accordance with the fundamental principles of their legal systems, shall cooperate with each other and with the relevant international and regional organizations in the promotion and formulation of the measures referred to in this Article. Such collaboration may include participation in international programs and projects designed to prevent corruption.

Article 6
Corruption prevention body or bodies

1. Each State Party shall, in accordance with the fundamental principles of its legal system, ensure that one or more bodies, as appropriate, are charged with preventing corruption with measures such as:

(a) the implementation of the policies referred to in Article 5 of this Convention and, where appropriate, the supervision and co-ordination of the practice of such policies;

(b) increasing and disseminating knowledge on the prevention of corruption.

2. Each State Party shall accord to the organ or bodies referred to in paragraph 1 of this Article the necessary independence, in accordance with the fundamental principles of its legal system, so that they may carry out their functions in a without any undue influence. They shall provide them with the material resources and specialized staff required, as well as the training that such personnel may require for the performance of their duties.

3. Each State Party shall communicate to the Secretary-General of the United Nations the name and address of the authority (ies) which may assist other States Parties in formulating and implementing concrete measures to prevent corruption.

Article 7 Public Sector

1. Each State Party, when appropriate and in accordance with the fundamental principles of its legal system, shall endeavor to adopt systems for convening, hiring, retaining, promoting and retiring public officials and, when it does so, other public officials shall not - or maintain and strengthen such systems. These:

(a) shall be based on principles of science and transparency and objective criteria such as merit, equity and fitness;

(b) shall include appropriate procedures for the selection and training of public office holders who consider themselves to be especially vulnerable to corruption and, where appropriate, for the rotation of such persons in other positions;

(c) promote adequate remuneration and fair pay scales, taking into account the level of economic development of the State Party;

(d) Promote training and capacity-building programs to enable them to meet the requirements of correct, honorable and owing performance and provide them with specialized and appropriate training to make them more aware corruption risks inherent in the performance of their functions. Such programs may refer to codes or standards of conduct in the relevant fields.

2. Each State Party shall also consider the possibility of adopting appropriate legislative and administrative measures, consistent with the objectives of this Convention and in accordance with the fundamental principles of its domestic law, to establish criteria for candidacy and election to public office.

3. Each State Party shall consider the possibility of adopting appropriate legislative and administrative measures, consistent with the objectives of this Convention and in accordance with the fundamental principles of its domestic law, to increase transparency regarding the funding of candidatures to elective public offices and, when appropriate, regarding the funding of political parties.

4. Each State Party shall, in accordance with the principles of its domestic law, seek to adopt systems to promote transparency and prevent conflicts of interest, or to maintain and strengthen such systems.

Article 8
Codes of conduct for civil servants

1. In order to combat corruption, each State Party shall, in accordance with the fundamental principles of its legal system, promote, among other things, integrity, honesty and responsibility among its public servants.

2. In particular, each State Party shall endeavor to apply, in its own institutional and legal systems, codes or standards of conduct for the correct, honorable and due fulfillment of public functions.

3. In order to implement the provisions of this Article, each State Party, when conducting and in accordance with the fundamental principles of its legal system, shall take note of the relevant initiatives of regional, interregional and multilateral conventions, such as the International Code of Conduct for Public Officials, contained in the annex to General Assembly resolution 51/59 of 12 December 1996.

4. Each State Party shall also consider, in accordance with the fundamental principles of its domestic law, the possibility of establishing measures and systems to facilitate public officials to report any act of corruption to the

competent authority when they become aware of them in the exercise of their functions.

5. Each State Party shall endeavor, when and in accordance with the fundamental principles of its domestic law, to establish measures and systems to require public officials to make statements to the competent authorities regarding, inter alia, their external activities and with jobs, investments, assets and gifts or important benefits that may give rise to a conflict of interest relating to their duties as public servants.

6. Each State Party shall consider adopting, in accordance with the fundamental principles of its domestic law, disciplinary or other measures against any civil servant who violates codes or standards established in accordance with this article.

Article 9
Public procurement and public farm management

1. Each State Party shall, in accordance with the fundamental principles of its legal system, adopt the necessary measures to establish appropriate public procurement systems, based on transparency, competence and objective criteria for decision-making, among other things, to prevent corruption. Such systems, where appropriate minimum values may be taken into account, should address, inter alia:

(a) the public dissemination of information on public procurement procedures and contracts, including information on bids and relevant or timely information on the award of contracts, so that potential bidders have sufficient time to prepare and submit bids;

b) The prior formulation of the terms of participation, including selection and award criteria and bidding rules, as well as their publication;

(c) the application of objective and predetermined criteria for the adoption of decisions on public procurement in order to facilitate the subsequent verification of the correct application of the rules or procedures;

(d) an internal review mechanism, including a system and appeal, to ensure remedies and legal remedies if the rules or procedures established under this paragraph are not respected;

(e) where appropriate, the adoption of measures to regulate matters relating to public procurement staff, in particular declarations of relative interest for certain public contracts, pre-selection procedures and training requirements.

2. Each State Party shall, in accordance with the fundamental principles of its legal system, adopt appropriate measures to promote transparency and accountability in the management of public finances. Such measures shall include, inter alia:

(a) procedures for the adoption of the national

nal;

(b) the timely submission of information on expenditure and tickets;

(c) a system of accounting and auditing standards, yes as the corresponding supervision;

(d) risk management and risk management systems and internal trolley; and

(e) Where appropriate, the adoption of corrective in case of non-compliance with the requirements set out in this paragraph.

3. Each State Party shall, in accordance with the fundamental principles of its domestic law, adopt such measures as are necessary in civil and administrative spheres to preserve the integrity of books and accounting, financial or other expense-related records and to prevent the falsification of these documents.

Article 10 Public information

Taking into account the need to combat corruption, each State Party shall, in accordance with the fundamental principles of its domestic law, adopt such measures as may be necessary to increase transparency in its public administration, including its organization, functioning and decision-making processes, when to proceed. These measures may include, inter alia:

(a) the introduction of procedures or regulations enabling the general public to obtain information on the organization, functioning and procedures for the adoption of decisions of its public administration, with due respect for the protection of privacy and personal documents, on the decisions and legal acts of the public;

(b) the simplification of administrative procedures, where appropriate, in order to facilitate public access to the decision-making authorities; and

c) The publication of information, which may include periodic reports on the risks of corruption in the public administration.

Article 11
Measures relating to the judiciary and public ministry

1. Bearing in mind the independence of the judiciary and

decisive role in the fight against corruption, each State Party, in accordance with the fundamental principles of its without prejudice to the independence of the judiciary, shall take measures to enhance integrity and avoid any opportunity for corruption among members of the judiciary. Such measures may include rules governing the conduct of members of the judiciary.

2. Measures similar to those adopted in paragraph 1 of this Article may be formulated and applied in the public prosecutor's office in States Parties where that institution is not a member of the judiciary but enjoys similar independence.

Article 12 Private Sector

1. Each State Party shall, in accordance with the fundamental principles of its domestic law, adopt measures to prevent corruption and improve accounting and auditing standards in the private sector and, where

appropriate, provide for civil, administrative or penal sanctions and dispatching, proportionate and dissuasive in the event of non-compliance.

2. Measures taken to achieve these objectives may include, inter alia:

(a) promote cooperation between law enforcement agencies and relevant private entities;

b) To promote the formulation of norms and procedures with the objective of safeguarding the integrity of the relevant private entities, including codes of conduct for the correct, honorable and due exercise of commercial activities and of all relevant provisions and for the prevention of interests, as well as to promote the use of good business practices between companies and contractual relations between companies and the State;

(c) to promote transparency between private entities, including, where appropriate, measures relating to the identification of legal and physical persons involved in the establishment and management of undertakings;

(d) to prevent misuse of procedures governing private entities, including the granting of subsidies and licenses by public authorities for commercial activities;

(e) Preventing conflicts of interest by imposing appropriate restrictions, for a reasonable period, on the professional activities of former civil servants or on the hiring of public servants by the private sector after their resignation or retirement when such activities or hiring are directly related to the functions performed or supervised by these public officials during their tenure in office;

f) Ensure that private companies, having their structure and size, have their own internal accounting controls to help prevent and detect acts of corruption and so that the accounts and financial statements required of these companies are subject to appropriate auditing and certification procedures;

3. In order to prevent corruption, each State Party shall adopt such measures as may be necessary in accordance with its internal laws and regulations

relating to the maintenance of books and records, the disclosure of financial statements and the accounting and auditing standards, to prohibit the following acts committed in connection with the commission of any of the offenses qualified in accordance with this Convention:

a) The establishment of accounts not registered in books;

b) The performance of transactions not recorded in books or badly specified;

c) The recording of nonexistent expenses;

d) The judgment of expenses in the books of account with an incorrect indication of its objective;

e) The use of false documents; and

f) The deliberate destruction of accounting documents before the period established by law.

4. Each State Party shall make a tax deduction in respect of expenses which may constitute bribery, which is one of the elements constituting the offenses established in accordance with Articles 15 and 16 of this Convention and, where applicable, other expenditure which has the purpose of promoting corrupt behavior.

Article 13 Participation of society

1. Each State Party shall take appropriate measures, within the limits of its capabilities and in accordance with the fundamental principles of its domestic law, to encourage the active participation of persons and groups not belonging to the public sector, such as civil society, non-governmental organizations, community-based organizations, the prevention and fight against corruption, and to raise public awareness of the existence, causes and seriousness of corruption, as well as the threat it poses. Such participation should be made with measures such as:

a) Increase transparency and promote the contribution of citizenship to decision-making processes;

b) Ensure public access to information;

c) Carry out public information activities to promote intransigence against corruption, as well as public education programs, including school and university programs;

d) Respect, promote and protect the freedom to seek, receive, publish and disseminate information on corruption. Such freedom may be subject to certain restrictions, which shall be expressly qualified by law and are necessary to: (i) Ensure respect for the rights or reputations of others; (ii) safeguard national security, public order, or public health or morals.

2. Each State Party shall take appropriate measures to ensure that the public is aware of the relevant anti-corruption bodies referred to in this Convention and shall facilitate access to such bodies, where appropriate, for the denunciation, including anonymity, of any incidents that may be considered to constitute an offense in accordance with this Convention.

Article 14
Measures to prevent money laundering

1. Each State Party shall:

(a) lay down a broad set of internal rules and regulations for the supervision of banks and non-bank financial institutions, including natural or legal persons providing official or informal money transfer services and, where appropriate, other organs located within its jurisdiction that are particularly suspected of being used for money laundering in order to prevent and detect all forms of money laundering, and in such a regiment the requirements relating to customer identification and, when to proceed from the final beneficiary to the establishment of records and to the reporting of suspicious transactions;

(b) ensure, without prejudice to the application of Article 46 of this Convention, that the authorities responsible for administering, regulating and enforcing the law and other authorities responsible for combating money laundering (including, where applicable, national law, judicial authorities) are able to cooperate and exchange information at the national and international levels, in accordance with the conditions laid down in domestic law, and to this end will consider establishing a financial intelligence department serving as a national center to compile, analyze and disseminate information on possible money laundering activities.

2. States Parties shall consider applying feasible measures to detect and monitor the cross-border movement of personnel and relevant negotiable instruments subject to safeguards ensuring the proper use of information and without restricting in any way the movement of persons. capitals. Such measures may include the requirement that individuals and commercial entities notify the cross-border transfers of large numbers of relevant staff and negotiable securities.

3. States Parties shall consider applying appropriate and feasible measures to require financial institutions, including money remitters, to:

a) Include in the forms of electronic transfer of funds and related messages accurate and valid information about the sender;

b) Maintain this information throughout the operation cycle; and

(c) to examine more closely transfers of funds which do not contain complete information about the sender. 4. In establishing internal rules of regulations and supervision in accordance with this Article, and without prejudice to any other article of this Convention, it is recommended that States Parties use the relevant initiatives of organizations as guides regional, interregional and multilateral agreements to combat money laundering.

5. States Parties shall endeavor to establish and promote to see co-operation at the global, regional, subregional and bilateral levels between law enforcement, law enforcement and financial regulation to combat money laundering.

Chapter III Penalty and law enforcement

Article 15
Bribery of national civil servants

Each State Party shall adopt such legislative and other measures as may be necessary to qualify as an offense when committed intentionally:

a) The promise, offer or concession to a public official, directly or indirectly, of an undue benefit that results in his or her own benefit or that of another person or entity with which such employee acts or refrains to act in the fulfillment of their official duties;

b) The solicitation or acceptance by a public official, directly or indirectly, of an undue for his own benefit or that of another person or entity so that such employee acts or refrains from acting in the performance of his official duties.

Article 16

Bribery of foreign public officials and officials of public international organizations

1. Each State Party shall adopt such legislative and other measures as may be necessary to qualify as a criminal offense, when committed intentionally, the promise, offering or grant, directly or indirectly, to a foreign public official or an international public organization of an undue benefit that results in its own or another person's or entity's benefit or that such employee acts or refrains from acting in the exercise of his or her functions to obtain or maintain any co- mercial or other undue advantage in connection with the performance of international business activities.

2. Each State Party shall consider adopting such legislative and other measures as may be necessary to qualify as a criminal offense, when committed intentionally, the request or acceptance by a foreign public official or official of a public international organization, in a direct manner or indirectly, an undue benefit that results in the benefit of itself or that

of another person or entity, with the proviso that such employee acts or refrains from acting in the exercise of his official duties.

Article 17
Embezzlement or embezzlement, misappropriation or other misuse of property by a public official

Each State Party shall adopt such legislative and other measures as may be necessary to qualify as an offense, when committed intentionally, embezzlement or embezzlement, misappropriation or other diversion of public or private assets or funds, or anything of value that has been attached to the employee by virtue of his position.

Article 18
Trafficking

Each State Party shall consider adopting such legislative and other measures as may be necessary to qualify as an offense when committed intentionally:

a) The promise, offer or concession to a public servant or to any other person, directly or indirectly, of an undue benefit, with the public official or person abusing his or her actual influence or supposed to obtain from an administration or authority of the State Party an undue benefit resulting in the benefit of the original instigator of the act or any other person;

b) The solicitation or acceptance by a public official or any other person, directly or indirectly, of an undue benefit that results in his or her own benefit or that of another person, such that the public official or the person abuses of his or her actual or alleged inability to obtain undue benefit from an administration or authority of the State Party.

Article 19
Abuse of duties

Each State Party shall consider the possibility of adopting such legislative and other measures as may be necessary to qualify as an offense, when committed intentionally, the abuse of office or position, that is, the performance or omission of an act, in violation of law by a public official in the performance of his or her duties with a view to obtaining undue benefit for himself or for another person or entity.

Article 20
Illegal enrichment

Subject to its constitution and to the fundamental principles of its legal system, each State Party shall consider the possibility of adopting such legislative and other measures as may be necessary to qualify as a criminal offense, intentionally, unlawful enrichment, that is, the significant increase in the assets of a public official relating to his legitimate income which can not reasonably be justified by him.

Article 21
Bribery in the private sector

Each State Party shall consider adopting such legislative and other measures as may be necessary to qualify as an offense when committed intentionally in the course of economic, financial or commercial activities:

a) The promise, offer or concession, directly or indirectly, to a person who directs a private sector entity or performs any function in it, an undue benefit that is for his own benefit or that of another person, inasmuch as, absent from the duty inherent in its functions, it acts or refrains from acting;

b) The solicitation or acceptance, directly or indirectly, by a person who directs a private sector entity or performs any function in it, of an undue benefit that flows for his own benefit or that of another person, with or that, absent from the duty inherent in its functions, acts or abstains from acting.

Article 22
Embezzlement or embezzlement of assets in the private sector

Each State Party shall consider the possibility of adopting such legislative and other measures as may be necessary to qualify as a criminal offense when committed intentionally in the course of economic, financial or commercial activities, embezzlement or embezzlement by a person directing an entity of the private sector or performs any function therein, of any assets, funds or private securities or of any other thing of value that has been attached to that person by virtue of his position.

Article 23
Product Laundering

1. Each State Party shall adopt, in accordance with the fundamental principles of its domestic law, such legislative and other measures as may be necessary to qualify as an offense when committed intentionally:

(a) (i) The conversion or transfer of property, provided that such property is the proceeds of crime, for the purpose of concealing or concealing the illicit origin of the property and assisting any person involved in the commission of the offense in order to the legal consequences of their actions;

ii) The concealment or dissimulation of the true nature, origin, situation, disposition, movement or ownership of goods or the legitimate right to them, knowing that such goods are products of crime;

b) Subject to the basic concepts of its legal system: i) The acquisition, possession or use of assets, knowing at the time of receipt that they are the proceeds of crime; (ii) The participation in the commission of any of the offenses qualified under this Article, as well as the association and conspiracy to commit them, the attempt to commit them and the aid, incitement, facilitation and counseling with a view to its practice.

2. For the nodes of application or implementation of paragraph 1 of this Article:

(a) Each State Party shall ensure that paragraph 1 of this Article applies to the widest possible range of determinant offenses;

(b) Each State Party shall include, as a minimum, a broad range of offenses which are qualified in accordance with this Convention;

(c) For the purposes of sub-paragraph (b) above, the following offenses shall include offenses committed both within and outside the jurisdiction of the State Party concerned. Nevertheless, offenses committed outside the jurisdiction of a State Party shall constitute a predicate offense, provided that the corresponding act is offense under the domestic law of the State in which it was committed and thus constitutes an offense under the domestic law of the State Party implementing or implementing this article if the offense had been committed there;

(d) Each State Party shall provide the Secretary-General of the United Nations with a copy of its laws designed to give effect to this Article and any subsequent amendment thereto in accordance with such laws;

(e) If the fundamental principles of the domestic law of a State Party so require, it may be provided that the offenses set forth in paragraph 1 of this Article shall not apply to persons who have committed the predicate offense.

Article 24
Cover-up

Without prejudice to Article 23 of this Convention, each State Party shall consider adopting such legislative and other measures as may be necessary to qualify the offense when committed intentionally after the commission of any of the offenses in accordance with this Convention but without their participation therein, the encroachment or continuous retention of property on the understanding that such property is the proceeds of any of the offenses qualified in accordance with this Convention.

Article 25
Obstruction of justice

Each State Party shall adopt such legislative and other measures as may be necessary to qualify as an offense when committed intentionally:

(a) The use of physical force, threats or intimidation, or the proclamation, offering or granting of undue advantage to induce a person to give false testimony or to obstruct the provision of testimony or the taking of evidence in proceedings relating to the commission of offenses established in accordance with that Convention;

(b) The use of physical force, threats or intimidation to obstruct the performance of the judicial functions of a court or law enforcement officer in connection with the commission of offenses in accordance with Convention. Nothing in this Article shall deprive the domestic legislation of States Parties which have legislation protecting other categories of public servants.

Article 26
Liability of legal persons

1. Each State Party shall take such measures as may be necessary, in accordance with its legal principles, in order to establish the liability of legal persons for their participation in offenses which are qualified in accordance with this Convention.

2. Subject to the legal principles of the State Party, the liability of legal persons may be criminal, civil or administrative.

3. Such liability shall be without prejudice to the criminal liability of individuals who have committed the offenses.

4. Each State Party shall in particular ensure that criminal or non-criminal sanctions and penalties, proportionate and dissuasive, including monetary sanctions, are imposed on legal persons considered liable pursuant to this Article.

Article 27
Participation or attempt

1. Each State Party shall adopt such legislative and other measures as may be necessary to qualify as a criminal offense, in accordance with its domestic law, any form of participation, whether as an accomplice, collaborator or instigator, in a qualifying offense with this Convention.

2. Each State Party may adopt such legislative and other measures as may be necessary to qualify as an offense, in accordance with its domestic law, any attempt to commit an offense in accordance with this Convention.

3. Each State Party may adopt such legislative and other measures as may be necessary to qualify as a criminal offense, in accordance with its domestic law, the preparation for the commission of a misdemeanor in accordance with this Convention.

Article 28
Knowledge, intention and purpose as elements of a crime

The knowledge, intention or purpose required as elements of an offense qualified under this Convention may be inferred from factual factual circumstances.

Article 29
Prescription

Each State Party shall establish, when in accordance with its domestic law, a broad limitation period for initiating proceedings for any of the offenses qualified under this Convention and shall establish a longer period or shall interrupt the limitation period when the presumed offender evaded the administration of justice.

Article 30
Procedure, sentence and sanctions

1. Each State Party shall punish the commission of offenses established in accordance with this Convention with penalties which take into account the seriousness of such offenses.

2. Each State Party shall adopt such measures as may be necessary to establish or maintain, in accordance with its legal system and constitutional principles, an appropriate balance between any immunities or jurisdictional prerogatives granted to its civil servants for the fulfillment of its obligations. functions and the possibility, if necessary, of effectively carrying out the investigation, indictment and award of offenses qualified in accordance with this Convention.

3. Each State Party shall ensure that any discretionary legal powers available to it under its domestic law in respect of the indictment of persons

for crimes qualified under this Convention are exercised in order to give full force and effect to the measures taken to enforce law regarding these crimes, taking due account of the need to prevent them.

4. In the case of offenses established in accordance with this Convention, each State Party shall take the appropriate measures in accordance with its domestic law and with due regard to the rights of the defense, with a view to ensuring that, by imposing conditions in relation to the decision to grant freedom pending trial or appeal, there is a need to ensure that the accused is present in all subsequent criminal proceedings.

5. Each State Party shall take into account the seriousness of the relevant offenses when considering the possibility of granting early release or conditional release to persons who have been found guilty of such offenses.

6. Each State Party shall consider establishing, insofar as it is in accordance with the fundamental principles of its legal system, procedures under which a public official who is charged with an offense in accordance with this Convention may, where appropriate, be removed, suspended or transferred by the relevant authority, bearing in mind respect for the principle of the presumption of innocence.

7. When the seriousness of the offense does not justify and insofar as it is consistent with the fundamental principles of its legal system, each State Party shall consider the possibility of establishing procedures to disqualify, by judicial order or other appropriate means and for a period determined in its domestic law, persons convicted of offenses qualified under this Convention to:

a) To hold public office; and

b) To hold positions in a company wholly or partially owned by the State.

8. Paragraph 1 of this Article shall be without prejudice to the application of disciplinary measures by competent authorities against public officials.

9. Nothing in this Convention shall affect the principle that a description of the offenses qualified in accordance therewith and the applicable legal or

defense means or other legal principles governing the legality of conduct other than that reserved for legislation States Parties and that such offenses shall be prosecuted and punished in accordance with such legislation.

10. States Parties shall seek to promote the social reintegration of persons convicted of offenses qualified under this Convention.

Article 31
Preventive arrest, seizure and confiscation

1. Each State Party shall, to the greatest extent permitted by its domestic legal system, take such measures as may be necessary to authorize the conspiracy:

(a) the proceeds of a criminal offense under this Convention or of goods the value of which corresponds to that of the pro-duct;

(b) goods, equipment or other instruments used in or used for the commission of offenses established in accordance with this Convention.

2. Each State Party shall take such measures as may be necessary to enable the identification, tracing, freezing or seizure of any property referred to in paragraph 1 of this Article with a view to its eventual settlement.

3. Each State Party shall adopt, in accordance with its domestic law, such legislative and other measures as may be necessary to regulate the administration by the competent authorities of seized, seized property or scados included in paragraphs 1 and 2 of this Article.

4. Where the proceeds of crime have been partially or totally converted or converted into other goods, they shall be subject to the measures applicable to such proceeds in accordance with this Article.

5. When this proceeds of crime have been mixed with goods acquired from lawful sources, such property shall be the object of a conspiracy up to the estimated value of the mixed product, without prejudice to any other possibility of freezing or seizure.

6. Tickets and other benefits derived from the proceeds of crime, of goods in which such proceeds or assets have been converted or converted to such proceeds of crime shall also be subject to the measures provided for in this Article, in the same manner and to the same degree as the proceeds of crime.

7. For the purposes of this Article and of Article 55 of this Convention, each State Party shall provide its courts or other competent authority with the power to order the production or presentation of bank, financial or commercial documents. The States Parties may not refrain from applying the provisions of this paragraph by relying on banking secrecy.

8. States Parties may consider the possibility of requiring a delinquent to demonstrate the lawful origin of the alleged offense of offense or other property exposed to the con insofar as it conforms to the fundamental principles of its legislation and the nature of the judicial process or other proceedings.

9. The provisions of this Article shall not be construed to prejudice the right of third parties acting in good faith.

10. Nothing in the present article shall affect the principle that the measures provided for therein shall cease and shall apply in accordance with and subject to the domestic law of the States Parties.

Article 32
Protection of witnesses, experts and victims

1. Each State Party shall take appropriate measures, in accordance with its domestic legal system and within its means, to provide effective protection against witnesses and witnesses of any crimes of in accordance with this Convention, as well as, when appropriate, their families and other persons close to them.

2. The measures provided for in paragraph 1 of this Article may consist, inter alia, without prejudice to the rights of the accused and including the right of procedural guarantees, in:

(a) establish procedures for the physical protection of such persons, including, as far as is necessary and possible, their removal, and, where appropriate, permit the total or partial prohibition of disclosing information on their identity and whereabouts;

b) Establish evidentiary standards that allow witnesses and experts to testify without endangering the safety of such persons, for example by accepting testimony through communication technologies such as video conferencing or other appropriate means.

3. States Parties shall consider the possibility of concluding agreements or treaties with other States for the removal of persons referred to in paragraph 1 of this Article.

4. The provisions of this Article shall also apply to victims to the extent that they are witnesses.

5. Each State Party shall, subject to its domestic law, allow the views and concerns of victims at appropriate stages of criminal proceedings against criminals to be presented and considered without detracting from the rights of the defense.

Article 33
Protection of whistleblowers

Each State Party shall consider the possibility of incorporating in its domestic legal system appropriate measures to provide protection against any unfair treatment of persons to report to the competent authorities, in good faith and on reasonable grounds, any facts relating to the offenses established in accordance with this Convention.

Article 34
Consequences of acts of corruption

With due regard to rights acquired in good faith by third parties, each State Party shall, in accordance with the fundamental principles of its domestic law, adopt measures to eliminate the consequences of acts of corruption. In this context, States Parties may consider corruption to be a relevant factor in legal proceedings designed to nullify or render ineffective a contract or to revoke a concession or other similar instrument, or to take any other corrective action.

Article 35
Indemnification for damages and losses

Each State Party shall take such measures as may be necessary in accordance with the principles of its domestic law to ensure that entities or persons harmed as a result of an act of corruption have the right to bring legal action against those responsible damages for damages.

Article 36
Specialized authorities

Each State Party, in accordance with the fundamental principles of its legal system, shall ensure that it has one or more organs or persons specialized in the fight against corruption through law enforcement. Such body (ies) or persons shall enjoy the necessary independence, in accordance with the fundamental principles of the State party's legal system, so that they can carry out their duties effectively and without undue pressure. Such persons or the staff of such body (s)adequate training and adequate resources for the performance of their duties.

Article 37
Cooperation with Law Enforcement Authorities

1. Each State Party shall take appropriate measures to re-establish persons who participate or have participated in the commission of offenses in accordance with this Convention, which provide the competent authorities with investigative and evidentiary information and and to provide them with effective and concrete aid to help deprive criminals of the proceeds of crime and to recover such proceeds.

2. Each State Party shall consider the possibility of providing, in appropriate cases, for the mitigation of punishment of any accused person who provides substantial cooperation in the investigation or prosecution of offenses qualified under this Convention.

3. Each State Party shall consider the possibility of providing, in accordance with the fundamental principles of its domestic law, for the grant of judicial immunity to any person who provides substantial cooperation in the investigation or prosecution of offenses qualified in accordance with this Convention.

4. The protection of such persons shall be *mutatis mutandis* as provided for in Article 32 of this Convention.

5. When the persons referred to in paragraph 1 of this Article are in a State Party and are able to provide substantial cooperation to the competent authorities of another State Party, the States Parties concerned may consider concluding treaties or agreements in in accordance with its domestic law, with respect to the possible concession by that Participating Party of the treatment provided for in paragraphs 2 and 3 of this Article.

Article 38
Cooperation between national bodies

Each State Party shall take such measures as may be necessary, in accordance with its domestic law, to establish cooperation between, on the one hand, its public bodies and its civil servants and, on the other, its organs charged with investigating and prosecuting crimes. Such cooperation may include:

(a) inform the latter bodies, at the initiative of the State Party, where it has reasonable grounds to suspect that any of the crimes qualified in accordance with Articles 15, 21 and 23 of this Convention have been committed; or

(b) provide such bodies with all necessary information upon request.

Article 39
Cooperation between national agencies and the private sector

1. Each State Party shall take such measures as may be necessary, in accordance with its domestic law, to establish cooperation between national investigation agencies and the public prosecution service on the one hand

and private sector entities in particularly financial institutions, on the other, in matters relating to the commission of offenses in accordance with this Convention.

2. Each State Party shall consider making it possible for its citizens and other persons residing in its territory to report to the national investigative bodies and to the public prosecutor the commission of any offense established in accordance with this Convention.

Article 40 Bank secrecy

Each State Party shall ensure that, in the case of national criminal investigations of offenses qualified under this Convention appropriate mechanisms to remove any obstacles that may arise as a result of the application of banking secrecy legislation.

Article 41
Criminal background

Each State Party may adopt such legislative or other measures as may be necessary to take into account, under such conditions and for such persons as it may deem appropriate, any prior declaration of guilt of a presumed criminal in another State to use such information in criminal offenses relating to offenses qualified under this Convention.

Article 42
Jurisdiction

1. Each State Party shall take such measures as may be necessary to establish its jurisdiction over offenses established in accordance with this Convention when:

a) The offense is committed in its territory; or

(b) The offense is committed on board a vessel which identifies that State or an aircraft registered under its laws at the time of its practice.

2. Subject to article 4 of this Convention, a State Party may also establish its jurisdiction to hear such offenses when:

a) The offense is committed against one of its citizens;

b) The offense is committed by one of its citizens or by a foreigner who is resident in its territory;

(c) The offense is one of the offenses qualified in accordance with subparagraph (b) (ii) of paragraph 1 of Article 23 of this Convention and committed outside its territory with a view to practicing, within its territory, (a) or "(i)" of part (b) of paragraph 1 of Article 23 of this Convention; or

(d) The offense is committed against the State Party.3. For the purposes of Article 44 of this Convention, each State Party shall take such measures as may be necessary to establish jurisdiction over offenses established in accordance with this Convention when the presumed criminal is present in its territory and the State Party does not extradite him because he is one of its citizens.

4. Each State Party may also take such measures as may be necessary to establish its jurisdiction over the offenses set forth in this Convention where the criminal budget is in its territory and the State Party does not extradite it.

5. If a State Party exercising its jurisdiction in accordance with paragraphs 1 or 2 of this Article is notified, or otherwise becomes aware, that other States Parties are conducting an investigation, prosecution or judicial proceeding concerning the same facts, the competent authorities of those States Parties shall consult, as appropriate, to coordinate their measures.

6. Without prejudice to the rules of general international law, this Convention shall not preclude the exercise of the criminal jurisdiction established by the States Parties in accordance with their domestic laws.

Chapter IV
International cooperation

Article 43
International cooperation

1. States Parties shall cooperate in criminal matters in accordance with Articles 44 to 50 of this Convention. Where appropriate and consistent with its domestic legal order, States Parties shall consider providing assistance in investigations and procedures relating to civil and administrative matters relating to corruption.

2. In matters of international cooperation, where dual criminality is a requirement, it shall be deemed to be whether the conduct constituting the offense in respect of which assistance is sought is an offense under the law of both States Parties, regardless of whether the laws of the requested State Party include the offense in the same category or refer to it with the same terminology as the State Party.

Article 44
Extradition

1. This Article shall apply to all offenses qualified under this Convention where the person who is the subject of the request for extradition is in the territory of the requested State Party, provided that the offense for which it is requested that extradition be punishable under the domestic law of the requesting State Party and the requested State Party.

2. Without prejudice to paragraph 1 of this Article, States Parties whose legislation so permits may grant the extradition of a person for any of the offenses covered by this Convention which are not punishable under its own domestic law.

3. Where the request for extradition includes a number of offenses, at least one of which gives rise to extradition in accordance with the provisions of this Article and some do not give rise to extradition due to the period of deprivation of liberty which they tolerate but are related to offenses

qualified under this Convention, the requested State Party may also apply this Article in respect of such offenses.

4. Each of the offenses to which this article applies shall be deemed to be included among the crimes giving rise to extradition in any extradition treaty between the States Parties. They undertake to include such offenses as grounds for extradition in any extradition treaty between them. The States Parties whose legislation allows them, where this Convention provides a basis for extradition, shall not consider any of the offenses qualified under this Convention to be of a political nature.

5. If a State Party which extradites a treaty receives a request for extradition from another State Party with which it does not conclude a treaty of extradition, it may consider this Convention as the legal basis of the treaty. extradition in respect of the offenses to which this article applies.

6. Any State Party which makes extradition subject to the existence of a treaty shall:

(a) When depositing its instrument of ratification, acceptance or approval of this Convention or of accession thereto, inform the Secretary-General of the United Nations whether or not to consider this Convention as the legal basis for cooperation in this field. extradition in its relations with the other States Parties to this Convention; and

(b) If it does not regard this Convention as the legal basis for cooperation in the matter of extradition, it shall endeavor, when to proceed, to conclude extradition treaties with other States Parties to this Convention in order to implement this Article.

7. States Parties which do not submit extradition to the existence of a treaty shall recognize the offenses to which this article applies as the cause of extradition between them.

8. Extradition shall be subject to the conditions laid down in the domestic law of the requested State Party or in the applicable extradition treaties, including, inter alia, those relating to the requirement of a minimum

sentence for extradition and the grounds which the State Required party may incur extradition.

9. States Parties shall, in accordance with their domestic law, seek to expedite extradition procedures and to simplify the corresponding probative requirements in respect of any of the offenses to which this article applies.

10. With respect to the provisions of its domestic law and its extradition treaties, the requested State Party may, after having ascertained that the circumstances so justify and are of an urgent nature, and at the request of the requesting State Party, proceed detention of the person present in its territory whose extradition requests or adopts other appropriate measures to person in extradition proceedings.

11. A State Party in whose territory a criminal offender is found, if he does not extradite him when an offense to which this article applies because he is one of its citizens, shall be bound, when requested by the State party requesting extradition, to submit the case without undue delay to its competent authorities for the purposes of indictment. The said authorities shall take their decision and carry out their legal proceedings in the same manner as they would in respect of any other serious crime under the domestic law of that State Party. The States Parties concerned shall cooperate with each other, in particular with regard to procedural and evidentiary aspects, with a view to ensuring the knowledge of such actions.

12. Where the domestic law of a State Party only allows the extradition or otherwise of one of its nationals, the condition that that person be returned to that State Party in order to comply with the sentence imposed as a result of the trial by the State Party requesting extradition or surrender and that State Party and the State Party requesting extradition accept such option, as well as such other condition as they deem appropriate, such extradition or conditional surrender shall be sufficient for the fulfillment of the obligation set forth in the paragraph 11 of this Article.

13. If extradition requested for the purpose of serving a sentence is denied by the fact that the requested person is a citizen of the requested State Party, the requested State Party, if its domestic law authorizes and in accordance with the requirements of the aforementioned legislation, shall consider,

at the request of the requesting State Party, the possibility of enforcing the sentence imposed or the rest of the sentence in accordance with the domestic law of the requesting State Party.

14. At all stages of the proceedings, a fair treatment shall be guaranteed to any person against whom an investigation has been initiated in relation to any of the offenses to which this article applies, including the enjoyment of all rights and guarantees by the domestic law of the State Party in whose territory that person is located.

15. Nothing in this Convention shall be construed as imposing an obligation to extradite if the requested State Party has reasonable grounds to presume that the request was lodged with a view to prosecuting or punishing a person sex, race, religion, nationality, ethnic origin or political opinion or that their compliance would prejudice the position of that person for any of these reasons.

16. States Parties may not deny an extradition request solely because it is considered that the offense also involves tax matters.

17. Before denying extradition, the requested State Party shall consult the requesting State Party in order to give it ample opportunity to present its views and to provide information relevant to its allegation.

18. States Parties shall endeavor to conclude bilateral or multilateral agreements or treaties to carry out extradition or to increase their status.

Article 45
Transfer of persons sentenced to serve a sentence

States Parties may consider the possibility of concluding bilateral or multilateral agreements or treaties on the transfer to their territory of any person who has been sentenced to imprisonment or other deprivation of liberty for any of the offenses qualified in accordance with this Convention that he may serve his sentence there.

Article 46 Mutual legal assistance

1. States Parties shall provide each other with more extensive mutual legal assistance in investigations, prosecutions and prosecutions relating to offenses covered by this Convention.

2. Mutual legal assistance shall be provided to the greatest extent possible in accordance with the relevant laws, treaties, agreements and declarations of the requested State Party with respect to investigations, prosecutions and legal proceedings relating to the offenses of which a legal person may be in accordance with Article 26 of this Convention in the requesting State Party.

3. Mutual legal assistance provided in accordance with this Article may be requested for any of the following:

a) Receive testimonies or take testimony of people; b) Present judicial documents;

c) Carry out inspections, seizures and / or preventive

the

d) Examine objects and places;

(e) To provide information, evidence and tions of experts;

(f) Delivering originals or certified copies of documents, including public, banking and financial documentation, as well as the social or commercial documentation of mercantile companies;

g) Identify or locate the proceeds of crime, property, instruments and other elements for evidence;

(h) facilitate the voluntary attendance of persons to the requesting State Party;

(i) Provide any other assistance authorized under the domestic law of the requested State Party;

(j) Identify, seize on a precautionary basis and locate the proceeds of crime in accordance with the provisions of Chapter V of this Convention;

(l) to recover assets in accordance with the provisions of Chapter V of this Convention.

4. Without prejudice to domestic law, the competent authorities of a State Party may, without prior request, transmit information relating to criminal matters to a competent authority of another State Party if they believe that such information could assist the authority to undertake or successfully complete inquiries and prosecutions or could give rise to a petition made by the latter State Party in accordance with this Convention.

5. The transmission of information in accordance with paragraph 4 of this Article shall be without prejudice to inquiries and prosecutions in the State of the competent authorities which have provided the information. The competent authorities that receive the information must comply with all requests that their confidential nature be respected, even temporarily, or that restrictions on their use be imposed. However, it shall not prevent the receiving State Party from disclosing, in its actions, information that is an acquittal of an accused person. In such a case, the receiving State Party shall notify the transmitting State Party before disclosing such information and, if so requested, shall consult the transmitting State Party. If, in an exceptional case, it is not possible to report in advance, the receiving State Party shall promptly inform the transmitting State Party of such disclosure.

6. The provisions of this Article shall not affect the inherent obligations of other existing or future bilateral or multilateral treaties which govern, in whole or in part, mutual legal assistance.

7. Paragraphs 9 to 29 of this Article shall apply to requests made in accordance with this Article, where a treaty of mutual legal assistance is not established between the States Parties concerned. When such States Parties are bound by such a treaty, the corresponding provisions of such treaty shall apply, except when States Parties agree to apply paragraphs 9 to 29 of this Article instead. States Parties are urged to apply these paragraphs if cooperation is facilitated.

8. States Parties shall not invoke banking secrecy to deny mutual legal assistance in accordance with this Article.

9. (a) In responding to a request for assistance under this Article, in the absence of double criminality, the requested State Party shall take into account the status of this Convention as set forth in Article 1;

(b) States Parties may refuse to provide assistance in accordance with this article by invoking the absence of double criminality. Nevertheless, the requested State Party, when it is in conformity with the basic concepts of its legal system, shall provide assistance that does not involve coercive measures. Such assistance may be denied where the request involves de *minimis* matters or issues in respect of which cooperation or assistance requested is provided for under other provisions of this Convention;

(c) In the absence of double criminality, each State Party may consider adopting the measures necessary to enable it to render wider assistance in accordance with this Article.

10. A person who is detained or serving a sentence in the territory of a State Party and whose presence is requested by another State Party for identification purposes, to testify or to assist in some other way in obtaining of the evidence required for investigations, prosecutions or prosecutions relating to the offenses covered by this Convention may be transferred if the following conditions are met:

a) The person, duly informed, gives his free consent;

(b) The competent authorities of both States Parties shall agree, subject to such conditions as they may deem appropriate.

11. For the purposes of paragraph 10 of this Article:

(a) The State Party to which the person is transferred shall have the power and the obligation to hold him or her in custody, unless the State Party from which the person has been transferred requests or authorizes otherwise;

(b) The State Party to which the person is transferred shall comply without delay with its obligation to return it to the custody of the State

158Part of which has transferred it, as agreed in advance or otherwise by the competent authorities of both States Parties;

(c) The State Party to which the person is transferred may not require the State Party from which the person has been transferred to initiate extradition proceedings for its return;

(d) The time in which the person has been detained in the State Party to which the person was transferred shall be counted as part of the sentence to be served in the State Party from which the person was transferred.

12. Unless the sending State Party of the person to be transferred in accordance with paragraphs 10 and 11 of this Article is in agreement, such person, whatever his or her nationality, shall not be prosecuted, detained, sentenced nor subject to any other restriction of his personal freedom in the territory of the State to which he was transferred in respect of acts, omissions or penalties prior to his leaving the territory of the sending State.

13. Each State Party shall designate a central authority responsible for receiving requests for mutual legal assistance and being allowed to comply with them or to transmit them to the competent authorities for its execution. Where a region or any special territory of a State Party has a separate registration of mutual legal assistance, the State Party may designate another central authority which shall perform the same function for that region or territory. The central authorities shall ensure the prompt and adequate compliance or transmission of the requests received. Where the central authority transmits the request to a competent authority for its execution, it shall encourage the prompt and proper execution of the request from the authority. Each State Party shall notify the Secretary-General of the United Nations at the time of depositing its instrument of ratification, acceptance or approval of this Convention or of accession thereto, the name of the central authority which has been designated for that purpose. Requests for mutual legal assistance and any other communication shall be transmitted to the central authorities designated by the States Parties. This provision shall not affect the legislation of any State Party to require

that such requests and communications be sent to it through the diplomatic channel and, in urgent circumstances, when the States Parties agree to it, through the conduct of the International Criminal Police Organization, if possible.

14. Requests shall be made in writing or, where possible, by any means capable of recording a written text in a language acceptable to the requested State Party. Under conditions allowing the said State Party to determine its authenticity. Each State Party shall notify the Secretary-General of the United Nations, at the time of deposit of its instrument of ratification, acceptance or approval of this Convention or accession thereto, of the language (s) which is (are) acceptable). In urgent situations, and when States Parties agree to it, requests may be made orally and must be made in writing without delay.

15. Any request for mutual legal assistance shall include the following:

a) The identity of the authority making the request;

(b) the subject matter and nature of the investigations, prosecutions and judicial proceedings to which the request refers and the name and functions of the authority responsible for carrying out such investigations, prosecutions or actions;

c) A summary of the relevant facts, except in the case of requests for the presentation of judicial documents;

(d) a description of the requested assistance and details of any particular procedure that the requesting State Party wishes it to apply;

e) If possible, the identity, status and nationality of each person concerned; and

f) The nature of the request for proof, information or performance.

16. The requested State Party may request additional information when necessary to comply with the request accordance with its domestic law or to facilitate such compliance.

17. All requests shall be complied with in accordance with the domestic law of the requested State Party and, to the extent that it does not contravene and is feasible in accordance with the procedures specified in the request.

18. Whenever it is possible and consistent with the fundamental principles of domestic law, when a person is in the territory of a State Party and has to testify or expert witness before the judicial authorities of another State Party, the first State Party at the request of the other, may allow the hearing to take place by videoconference if it is not possible or convenient for the person concerned to appear in person in the territory of the requesting State Party. States Parties may agree that a hearing by a judicial authority of the requesting State Party and which is assisted by a judicial authority of the requested State Party.

19. The requesting State Party shall not transmit or use, without the prior consent of the requested State Party, the information or evidence provided by the requested State for investigations, prosecutions or judicial proceedings other than those indicated in the request. Nothing in this paragraph shall prevent the requesting State Party from disclosing, in its actions, information or evidence that is the acquittal of an accused person. In the latter case, the requesting State Party shall notify the requested State Party before disclosing the information or evidence and, if so requested, shall consult the requested State Party. If, in an exceptional case, it can not be reported in advance, the requesting State Party shall promptly inform the requested State Party of such disclosure.

20. The requesting State Party may require the requested State Party to maintain confidentiality of the existence and content of the request, except to the extent necessary to comply with it. If the requested State Party can not maintain such confidentiality, it shall have the requesting State Party to know it immediately.

21. Mutual legal assistance may be denied:

(a) where the request is not in accordance with the provisions of this Article;

(b) when the requested State Party considers that compliance with the request would jeopardize its sovereignty, security, public order or other fundamental interests;

(c) where the domestic law of the requested State Party prohibits its authorities from acting in the manner requested in respect of a similar offense if it has been the subject of investigations, prosecutions or legal proceedings in the exercise of its own jurisdiction;

(d) When complying with the request is contrary to the legal order of the requested State Party in respect of mutual legal assistance.

22. States Parties may not deny a request for mutual legal assistance solely because they consider that the offense also involves tax matters.

23. Any denial of mutual legal assistance shall be duly substantiated.

24. The requested State Party shall comply with the request for mutual legal assistance as soon as possible and shall take full account, to the extent of its possibilities, of the time limits suggested by the requesting State Party and duly substantiated, preferably in the solicitation. The requesting State Party may request reasonable information on the status and progress of the measures taken by the requested State Party to comply with the petition. The requested State Party shall respond to reasonable requests made by the requesting State Party regarding the status and progress of the proceedings. The requesting State Party shall promptly inform the requested State Party when it no longer needs the requested assistance.

25. Mutual legal assistance may be modified by the requested State Party if it disturbs ongoing investigations, prosecutions or prosecutions.

26. Before denying a request made in accordance with paragraph 21 of this Article or modifying its accordance with paragraph 25 of this Article, the requested State Party shall consult the requesting State Party to consider whether it is possible to provide the requested assistance by submitting it to the conditions it deems necessary. If the requested State Party accepts assistance under these conditions, that State Party shall comply with the conditions imposed.

27. Without prejudice to the application of paragraph 12 of this Article, a witness, expert or other person who, at the request of the requesting State Party, agrees to testify in court or to collaborate in an investigation, prosecution or judicial action in the territory of the Requesting State, may not be indicted, detained, sentenced or subjected to any restriction of his or her personal freedom in that territory for acts, omissions or convictions prior to the time when he or she left the territory of the requested State Party. Such insurance shall cease when the witness, expert or other person has had, for a period of 15 (fifteen) consecutive days or during the period agreed between the States Parties after the date on which he has been informed that the judicial authorities no longer required his presence, the opportunity to leave the country and nevertheless voluntarily remained in that territory or returned to him freely after having abandoned him.

28. The ordinary expenses incurred in complying with the request shall be borne by the requested State Party, unless the States Parties concerned have agreed otherwise. Where substantial or extraordinary expenditures are required for this purpose, States Parties shall consult each other to determine the conditions under which the request shall be met and the manner in which the costs shall be borne.

29. The requested State Party:

(a) provide the requesting State Party with a copy of the documents and other documents or papers it has under its custody and which, in accordance with its domestic law, are accessible to the general public;

(b) May, at its discretion and subject to such conditions as it may deem appropriate, provide the requesting State Party a copy in whole or in part of official documents or other documents or papers held by them in their custody and which, according to their domestic legislation, are not accessible to the general public.

30. When necessary, States Parties shall consider the possibility of concluding bilateral or multilateral agreements or treaties which contribute to the achievement of the provisions of this Article and which lead to the implementation or strengthening of its provisions.

Article 47 Weakening of criminal proceedings

States Parties shall consider the possibility of weakening criminal prosecutions for indictment of a qualified offense under this Convention when it is considered that such a remission will benefit the proper administration of justice, particularly in cases involving several jurisdictions, with a view to concentrating the actions of the process.

Article 48
Cooperation in law enforcement

1. States Parties shall cooperate strictly, in accordance with their respective legal and administrative systems, with a view to increasing the effectiveness of law enforcement measures to combat offenses covered by this Convention. In particular, States Parties shall take measures and hunts to:

(a) to improve the channels of communication between its competent authorities, agencies and services and, where necessary, to establish them, and to facilitate the rapid and secure exchange of information on all aspects of the offenses covered by this Convention, if the States Parties concerned deem it opportune, on their links with other criminal activities;

(b) Cooperate with other States Parties in the conduct of inquiries concerning offenses covered by this Convention concerning: (i) Identity, whereabouts and activities of persons presumed to be involved in such offenses or the situation of other persons concerned; (ii) the movement of the proceeds of crime or property derived from the commission of such offenses; iii) The movement of goods, equipment or other instruments used or destined to practice these crimes.

(c) provide, where appropriate, the elements or quantities of substances required for analysis and investigation.

(d) exchange, where appropriate, information with other States Parties on the concrete means and methods employed for the commission of offenses covered by this Convention, including the use of false identities, falsified, altered or forged documents or other means of covering up activities linked to these crimes;

(e) Facilitate coordination and cooperation between its competent agencies, authorities and services and promote the exchange of personnel and other matters, including the designation of liaison officers subject to bilateral agreements or treaties between the States Parties concerned;

(f) exchange information and coordinate the administrative and other measures adopted for the prompt detection of the offenses covered by this Convention.

2. States Parties, with a view to giving effect to this Convention, shall consider the possibility of concluding bilateral or multilateral agreements or treaties on direct cooperation between their respective law enforcement agencies and, where such agreements or treaties already exist, improve them. In the absence of such agreements or treaties between the States Parties concerned, States Parties may consider that this Convention constitutes the basis for reciprocal co-operation in the field of law enforcement with respect to the offenses covered by this Convention. Where appropriate, States Parties shall take full advantage of agreements and treaties, including international or regional organizations, in order to enhance cooperation between their respective law enforcement agencies.

3. States Parties shall endeavor to cooperate to the extent possible to deal with offenses covered by this Convention which are committed through the use of modern technology.

Article 49 Joint investigations

States Parties shall consider the possibility of concluding bilateral or multilateral agreements or treaties by virtue of which, in relation to matters under investigation, prosecution or prosecution in one or more States, the competent authorities may establish joint investigative bodies. In the absence of such agreements or treaties, joint investigations may be carried out by agreement on a case-by-case basis. The States Parties concerned shall ensure that the sovereignty of the State Party in whose territory the investigation is carried out is fully respected.

Article 50
Special investigative techniques

1. In order to combat and actively engage in corruption, each State Party, to the extent that it allows it the fundamental principles of its domestic legal system and in accordance with the conditions prescribed by its domestic law, shall adopt such measures as may be necessary within its competent authorities in its territory, to supervised delivery and, where appropriate, other special investigative techniques such as electronic or other surveillance and secret operations, as well as admissibility of the evidence derived from such techniques in their courts.

2. For the purpose of investigating the offenses covered by this Convention, it is recommended that States Parties conclude, when appropriate, appropriate bilateral or multilateral agreements or treaties for the use of such special investigative techniques in the context of international cooperation. Such agreements or treaties shall be supported and implemented in full respect of the principle of sovereign equality of States and, in implementing them, the conditions contained therein shall be strictly limited.

3. In the absence of the agreements or treaties mentioned in paragraph 2 of this Article, any decision to resort to such special investigative techniques at international level shall be taken on a case-by-case basis and may, where necessary, take into account financial treaties and understandings concerning the exercise of jurisdiction by States Concerned.

4. Any decision to use internationally supervised delivery may, with the consent of the States Parties concerned, include the application of methods such as intercepting assets and funds, authorize them to proceed intact or withdraw or replace them all or part of them.

Chapter V Asset Recovery

Article 51 General provision

The restitution of assets under this Chapter is a fundamental principle of this Convention and the States Parties shall cooperate and assist each other in this regard.

Article 52
Prevention and detection of crime product transfers

1. Without prejudice to Article 14 of this Convention, each State Party shall take such measures as may be necessary, in accordance with its domestic law, to require financial institutions operating in its territory to see who the clients, take reasonable steps to determine the identity of the beneficial owners of funds deposited in large accounts, and intensify their scrutiny of any account requested or maintained in or by the name of persons performing or having performed eminent public functions and their family and close collaborators. This shall be reasonably structured so as to enable suspicious transactions to be discovered in order to inform the competent authorities and shall not be designed in such a way as to hinder or impede the normal course of business of financial institutions with their legitimate clientele.

2. In order to facilitate the implementation of the measures provided for in paragraph 1 of this article, each State Party shall, in accordance with its domestic legislation and drawing on relevant initiatives of its regional, interregional and multilateral organizations to combat money laundering, it should:

(a) lay down guidelines on the type of natural or legal persons whose accounts the financial institutions operating in its territory should subject to greater scrutiny, the types of accounts and transactions to which they should pay particular attention and the appropriate manner of opening accounts and to keep registers or records relating to them; and

(b) where appropriate, notify the financial institutions operating in its territory, at the request of another State Party or on its own initiative, of the identity of certain natural or legal persons whose accounts such institutions shall be subject to further scrutiny, in addition to which financial institutions can identify differently.

3. In the context of paragraph 2 (a) of this Article, each State Party shall implement measures to ensure that financial institutions maintain, for a suitable period of time, adequate records of the accounts and transactions relating to the persons referred to in paragraph 1. paragraph 1 of this

Article, which shall contain at least information concerning the identity of the customer and, as far as possible, the beneficiary.

4. In order to prevent and detect transfers of proceeds of crime under this Convention, each State Party shall take appropriate and effective measures to prevent, with the assistance of its regulatory and supervisory bodies, the establishment of banks that have no real presence and are not affiliated with a financial group subject to regulation. In addition, the possibility of requiring their financial institutions to refuse to enter into relations with such institutions as correspondent banks or to continue existing relationships and to refrain from establishing relations with foreign financial institutions their accounts to banks that have no real presence and are not affiliated with a regulated financial group.

5. Each State Party shall consider the possibility of establishing, in accordance with its domestic law, systems and funds for the dissemination of financial information to relevant public officials and shall apply appropriate sanctions for any non-compliance with the duty to report. Each State Party shall also consider adopting such measures as may be necessary to enable its competent authorities to share this information with the competent authorities of other States Parties if it is necessary to investigate, reclaim or recover the proceeds of crime qualified in accordance with this Convention.

6. Each State Party shall consider taking such measures as may be necessary, in accordance with its domestic law, to require relevant public officials who have any right or power of attorney or other authority over any account in a foreign country which declares their relationship with the account to the competent authorities and which leads to the proper registration of such account. These measures should include adequate penalties for any non-compliance.

Article 53
Measures for the direct recovery of property

Each State Party shall, in accordance with its domestic law:

(a) Take such measures as may be necessary to enable other States Parties to bring a civil action before their courts with a view to property or property acquired through the commission of an offense qualified in accordance with this Convention;

(b) take such measures as may be necessary to enable its courts to order those who have committed offenses qualified under this Convention to indemnify or reimburse for damages and losses to another State Party which has been adversely affected by these crimes; and

(c) Take such measures as may be necessary to enable its courts or its competent authorities, when they are to take decisions in respect of the property, which recognizes the legitimate right of ownership of another State Party over the acquired property through the commission of one of the offenses qualified in accordance with this Convention.

Article 54
Mechanisms for the recovery of goods through international cooperation for nsdeconsco

1. Each State Party shall provide mutual legal assistance in accordance with the provisions of Article 55 of this Convention relating to property acquired through the commission of any offense qualified in accordance with this Convention or relating thereto. offenses, in accordance with its domestic law:

(a) take such measures as may be necessary to enable its competent authorities to give effect to any order of detention ordered by a court of another State Party;

(b) take such measures as may be necessary for its competent authorities, where they have jurisdiction, to order the collection of such foreign-origin property in a sense relating to a money laundering offense or any other offense over which may have jurisdiction, or through other procedures authorized in its domestic legislation; and

(c) Consider taking such measures as may be necessary to enable the possession of such property without imprisonment in cases where the offender can not be indicted on grounds of death, escape or absence, or other appropriate cases.

2. Each State Party shall, in accordance with its domestic law, provide mutual legal assistance requested in accordance with paragraph 2 of Article 55 of this Convention:

(a) Take such measures as may be necessary for its competent authorities to effect the freezing or seizure of property in pursuance of a preventive arrest warrant or seizure ordered by a competent court or authority of a requesting State Party which constitute a reasonable basis for the requested State Party to consider that there are sufficient grounds for adopting such measures and that the assets would subsequently be the subject of a conspiracy order in accordance with the effects of subparagraph (a) present Article;

(b) Take such measures as may be necessary to enable its competent authorities to effect the freezing or seizure of property in pursuance of a request which provides a reasonable basis for the requesting State Party to consider that there are reasonable grounds for adopting such measures and that the goods would subsequently be the subject of a commercial order in accordance with the effects of part (a) of paragraph 1 of this Article; and

(c) Consider taking further steps to ensure that its competent authorities may preserve property for the purpose of contraction, for example on the basis of a foreign arrest warrant or imputation of criminal liability in connection with the acquisition of such property.

Article 55
International cooperation for business

1. States Parties which receive a request from another State Party having jurisdiction to hear one of the offenses qualified under this Convention for the purpose of confiscating proceeds of crime, property, equipment or other instrumentalities referred to in paragraph 1 of Article 31 of this Convention which are in its territory shall, to the greatest extent permitted by its domestic legal system:

a) Send the request to its competent authorities to obtain a control order which, in case of concession, will comply; or

(b) submit to its competent authorities, in order to comply with the request, a court order issued by a court situated in the territory of the requesting State Party in accordance with paragraph 1 of Article 31 and part (a) "Of paragraph 1 of Article 54 of this Convention insofar as it relates to the proceeds of crime, property, equipment or other instruments referred to in paragraph 1 of Article 31 which are in the territory of the requested State Party.

2. On the basis of the request made by another State Party having jurisdiction to hear one of the offenses established in accordance with this Convention, the requested State Party shall adopt measures for the identification, location and seizure preventive or seizure of the proceeds of crime, property, equipment or other instrumentalities referred to in paragraph 1 of this Convention with a view to its possible settlement, which shall be ordered by the requesting State Party or, if it involves a request submitted in accordance with paragraph 1 of this Article, the requested State Party.

3. The provisions of Article 46 of this Convention shall apply mutatis mutandis to this Article. In addition to the information indicated in paragraph 15 of Article 46, requests submitted pursuant to this Article shall contain the following:

(a) In the case of a request relating to part (a) of paragraph 1 of this Article, a description of the property susceptible to property, as well as, as far as possible, the situation and, where appropriate, the value estimate of property and an account of the facts on which the requesting State Party's request is based which are sufficiently explicit for the requested State Party to process the order in accordance with its domestic law;

(b) In the case of a request relating to part (b) of paragraph 1 of this Article, a copy acceptable to the a statement of the facts and information on the degree of execution requested to be given to the order, a statement indicating the measures taken by the requesting State Party on which the request is based, by the requesting State Party to give adequate notice to third parties in good faith and to ensure due process and a certificate that the order of the party is null and void;

(c) In the case of a request relating to paragraph 2 of this Article, a statement of the facts on which the requesting State Party is based and a description of the measures requested, as well as, when available, a copy acceptable to the the order in which the request is based.

4. The requested State Party shall adopt the decisions or measures provided for in paragraphs 1 and 2 of this Article in accordance with and subject to its domestic law and its rules of procedure or bilateral or multilateral agreements or treaties for which it may be the requesting State Party.

5. Each State Party shall provide the Secretary-General of the United Nations with a copy of its laws and regulations intended to give effect to this Article and of any subsequent amendments to such laws or regulations or a description thereof.

6. If a State Party chooses to subject the measures referred to in paragraphs 1 and 2 of this Article to the existence of a relevant treaty, that State Party shall treat this Convention as the necessary legal basis and its ability to comply this requirement.

7. The cooperation provided for in this Article may also be denied, or precautionary measures may be taken if the requested State Party does not receive adequate or timely evidence or if the goods are of scarce value.

8. Prior to lifting any interim measure taken pursuant to this Article, the requested State Party shall, whenever possible, give the requesting State Party the opportunity to state its reasons in favor of maintaining the measure in force.

9. The provisions of this Article shall not be construed to prejudice the rights of bona fide third parties.

Article 56
Special cooperation

Without prejudice to the provisions of its domestic law, each State Party shall endeavor to adopt such measures as may enable it to refer to another State Party which has not requested, without prejudice to its own investigations or legal proceedings, information on the proceeds of the offenses in accordance with the present Convention if it considers that the disclosure of such information may assist the receiving State Party in initiating or carrying out its investigations or prosecutions or that the information so facilitated could give rise to the State Party - shall submit a request in accordance with this Chapter of this Convention.

Article 57
Restitution and disposition of assets

1. Each State Party shall dispose of property which has been settled in accordance with the provisions of Articles 31 or 55 of this Convention, including restitution to its prior rightful owners in accordance with paragraph 3 of this Article, in accordance with provisions of this Convention and its domestic law.

2. Each State Party shall, in accordance with the fundamental principles of its domestic law, adopt such legislative and other measures as may be necessary to enable its competent authorities to reinstate confiscated property, request submitted by another State Party in accordance with this Convention, taking into account the rights of bona fide third parties.

3. In accordance with Articles 46 and 55 of this Convention and paragraphs 1 and 2 of this Article, the requested State Party shall:

(a) In the event of embezzlement or embezzlement of public funds or laundering of misappropriated public funds referred to in Articles 17 and 23 of this Convention, it shall reimburse the requesting State Party for goods conveyed when the collection has taken place in accordance with the provisions of Article 55 of this Convention and on the basis of the judgment handed down in the requesting State Party, a condition which may be waived by the requested State Party;

(b) In the case of the proceeds of any other offense covered by this Convention, it shall return to the requesting State Party property in accordance with article 55 of this Convention and on the basis of a judgment handed down in the requesting State Party, a condition which may be waived by the requested State Party and where the requesting State Party reasonably believes before the requested State Party its prior ownership of the disputed property or the requested State Party recognizes the damage caused to the requesting State Party as the basis for the restitution of property with scados;

(c) In all other cases, priority consideration shall be given to the restitution to the requesting State Party of the property in question, to the restitution of such property to its previous legitimate owners or to the compensation of the victims of the crime.

4. When proceeding, unless the States Parties otherwise decide, the requested State Party may deduct the reasonable expenses incurred in the course of investigations or judicial proceedings that have enabled the restitution or disposition of the property in accordance with the provisions in this Article.

5. In doing so, States Parties may also give special consideration to the possibility of concluding mutually acceptable agreements or treaties based on a particular case for the purpose of disposing of goods with goods.

Article 58
Department of Financial Intelligence

States Parties shall cooperate with each other to prevent and combat the transfer of proceeds of any of the offenses established in accordance with this Convention and to promote means of recovering the said product and for this purpose shall consider the possibility of establishing a financial intelligence department which shall be responsible for receiving, analyzing and making known to the competent authorities all information relating to suspicious financial transactions.

Article 59
Bilateral and multilateral agreements and treaties

States Parties shall consider the possibility of concluding bilateral or multilateral agreements or treaties with a view to increasing the scope of international cooperation provided in accordance with this Chapter of this Convention.

Chapter VI
Technical assistance and exchange of information

Article 60
Training and technical assistance

1. Each State Party shall, to the extent necessary, develop, develop or improve training programs specifically designed for the personnel of its services charged with the prevention and combating of corruption. These training programs may address, inter alia:

(a) Measures and measures to prevent, detect, investigate, punish and combat corruption, including the use of evidence-gathering and investigation methods;

b) Promotion of the capacity to formulate and plan a strategic anti-corruption policy;

(c) the training of competent authorities in the preparation of requests for mutual legal assistance which satisfy the requirements of this Convention;

d) Evaluation and strengthening of institutions, management of the public function and management of public nance, including public contracting, as well as the private sector;

(e) prevention and control of transfers of proceeds of any of the offenses qualified under this Convention and recovery of such proceeds;

(f) Detection and freezing of transfers of proceeds of any of the offenses qualified in accordance with this Convention;

(g) surveillance of the movement of proceeds of any of the offenses qualified under this Convention, as well as of the methods used for the transfer, concealment or concealment of such proceeds;

(h) Appropriate and appropriate legal and administrative mechanisms and methods to facilitate the return of proceeds of any of the offenses qualified under this Convention;

(i) methods used to protect victims and witnesses who cooperate with judicial authorities; and

(j) Training in national and international regulations and in languages.

2. To the best of their ability, States Parties shall consider providing the widest possible technical assistance, especially for developing countries, in their respective plans and programs to combat corruption, including material support and training in the areas referred to in paragraph 1 of this Article, as well as training and assistance and mutual exchange of experience and expertise, which will facilitate international cooperation among States Parties in the areas of extradition and mutual legal assistance.

3. States Parties shall, to the extent necessary, intensify efforts to optimize operational and capacity-building activities in international and regional organizations and within the framework of relevant bilateral or multilateral agreements or treaties.

4. States Parties shall consider, upon request, the possibility of assisting each other in conducting assessments, studies and investigations on the types, causes, effects and costs of corruption in their respective countries with a view to developing, with the participation of competent authorities and society, strategies and action plans against corruption.

5. In order to facilitate the recovery of the proceeds of any of the offenses qualified under this Convention, theStates Parties may cooperate by facilitating the names of the peers that may be useful in achieving this goal.

6. States Parties shall consider the possibility of organizing subregional, regional and international conferences and seminars to promote cooperation and technical assistance and to foster discussions on issues of mutual interest, including the special problems and needs of developing countries and countries with economies in transition.

7. States Parties shall consider the possibility of establishing voluntary mechanisms with a view to contributing to the efforts of developing countries and countries with economies in transition to implement this Convention through technical assistance programs and projects.

8. Each State Party shall consider making voluntary contributions to the United Nations Office on Drugs and Crime with a view to promoting, through the Office, programs and projects in developing countries with a view to implementing this Convention.

Article 61
Recompilation, exchange and analysis of information on corruption

1. Each State Party shall consider the possibility of analyzing, in consultation with experts, trends in corruption on its territory, as well as the circumstances in which corruption offenses are committed.

2. States Parties shall consider the possibility of developing and sharing, between themselves and through the action of international and regional organizations, statistics, analytical experience on corruption and information with a view to establishing, as far as possible, standards and methodologies, as well as information on acceptable practices to prevent and combat corruption.

3. Each State Party shall consider the possibility of ensuring its policies and measures in force aimed at combating corruption and assessing its effectiveness and science.

Article 62

Other measures: implementation of this Convention by means of economic development and technical assistance

1. States Parties shall adopt provisions consistent with the acceptable application of this Convention to the extent possible, through international cooperation, taking into account the adverse effects of corruption on society in general and on sustainable development in particular.

2. States Parties shall make concrete efforts, as far as possible and in a coordinated manner among themselves, as well as with international and regional organizations, in order to:

(a) intensify its cooperation in the various plans with developing countries with a view to strengthening their capacity to prevent and combat corruption;

(b) Increase financial and material assistance to support the efforts of developing countries to prevent and combat corruption and to assist them in the successful implementation of this Convention;

(c) Provide technical assistance to developing countries and countries with economies in transition to assist them in meeting their needs related to the implementation of this Convention. To this end, States Parties shall endeavor to make adequate and periodic voluntary contributions to an account specifically designated for that purpose in a United Nations funding mechanism. In accordance with their domestic law and with the provisions of this Convention, States Parties may also give special consideration to the possibility of entering into this account a percentage of the cash received or of the sum equivalent to the goods or proceeds of crime with accordance with the provisions of this Convention;

(d) To support and persuade other States Parties and financial institutions, as appropriate, to combine the efforts made in accordance with this Article, in particular by providing more modern training programs and equipment to developing countries and developing countries to help them achieve the objectives of this Convention.

3. These measures shall, as far as possible, not detract from existing external assistance commitments or other bilateral, regional or international financial cooperation agreements.

4. States Parties may conclude bilateral or multilateral agreements or treaties on material and logistic assistance, taking into account the financial arrangements necessary to give effect to international cooperation under this Convention and to prevent, detect and combat corruption.

Chapter VII
Enforcement mechanisms

Article 63
Conference of the States Parties to the present Convention

1. A Conference of States Parties to this Convention shall be established to improve the capacity of States Parties and cooperation between them to achieve the objectives set forth in this Convention and to promote and review their application.

2. The Secretary-General of the United Nations shall convene the Conference of the States Parties to this Convention not later than one year after the entry into force of this Convention. Thereafter, regular meetings of the Conference of States Parties shall be held in accordance with the rules of procedure adopted by the Conference.

3. The Conference of States Parties shall adopt the rules and regulations governing the implementation of the activities set out in this Article, including rules on the admission and participation of observers and the payment of expenses incurred in carrying out those activities.

4. The Conference of States Parties shall carry out activities, procedures and methods of work with a view to achieving the objectives set forth in paragraph 1 of this article, and in particular:

(a) facilitate the activities of States Parties in accordance with Articles 60 and 62 and Chapters II to V of this Convention, including by promoting the encouragement of voluntary contributions;

(b) Facilitate the exchange of information between the States Parties on the modalities and trends of corruption and on practices and hunts to prevent and combat it, as well as for the return of proceeds of crime, through, inter alia, publication of the relevant information referred to in this Article;

(c) cooperation with relevant international and regional organizations and mechanisms and non-governmental organizations;

(d) Make appropriate use of relevant information prepared by other international and regional mechanisms charged with combating and preventing corruption in order to avoid unnecessary duplication of activities;

(e) periodically review the implementation of this Convention by its States Parties;

(f) make recommendations to improve this Convention and its implementation;

(g) Take note of the technical assistance needs of States Parties with regard to the implementation of this Convention and recommend such measures as it deems necessary in this regard.

5. For the purposes of paragraph 4 of this Article, the Conference of the States Parties shall obtain the necessary knowledge of the measures adopted and the difficulties encountered by the States Parties in the implementation of this Convention through the information they provide and other the Conference of States Parties.

6. Each State Party shall provide the Conference of States Parties with information on its programs, plans and practices, as well as on the legislative and administrative measures taken to implement this Convention, as may be required by the Conference of States Parties. The Conference of States Parties shall endeavor to determine the most effective way to receive and process information, including information received from States Parties and competent international organizations. Approvals received from relevant non-governmental organizations duly accredited in accordance with procedures agreed by the Conference of States Parties may also be considered.

7. In accordance with paragraphs 4 to 6 of this Article, the Conference of States Parties shall, if it deems necessary, establish an appropriate mechanism or body to support the effective implementation of this Convention.

Article 64
Secretary

1. The Secretary-General of the United Nations shall provide necessary to the Conference of States Parties to this Convention.

2. The secretariat:

(a) assist the Conference of States Parties in carrying out the activities set forth in Article 63 of this Convention and shall organize the periods of sessions of the Conference of States Parties and shall provide them with the necessary services;

(b) Provide assistance to States Parties that request it in the information sub-office of the Conference of States Parties as provided for in paragraphs 5 and 6 of Article 63 of this Convention; and

(c) ensure the necessary coordination with the secretariats of other relevant international and regional organizations.

Chapter VIII
Provisions

Article 65
Application of the Convention

1. Each State Party shall, in accordance with the fundamental principles of its domestic law, adopt such measures as may be necessary, including legislative and administrative measures, to ensure fulfillment of its obligations under this Convention.

2. Each State Party may take more stringent or severe measures than those provided for in this Convention in order to prevent and combat corruption.

Article 66
Settlement of disputes

1. States Parties shall seek to resolve any dispute relating to the interpretation or application of this Convention by negotiation.

2. Any dispute between two or more States Parties concerning the interpretation or application of this Convention which can not be settled by negotiation within a reasonable time shall, at the request of one of these States Parties, be submitted to arbitration. If, six months after the date of the request for arbitration, those States Parties have not agreed on the organization of the arbitration, any of the States Parties may refer the dispute to the International Court of Justice upon request in accordance with the Statute of the Court.

3. Each State Party may at the time of ratification accept or approve this Convention or accede to it, declare that it does not consider itself bound by the paragraph of this Article. The other States Parties shall not be bound by paragraph 2 of this Article in respect of any State Party that has made such a reservation.

4. The State Party which has made a reservation in accordance with paragraph 3 of this Article may at any time withdraw this reservation by notifying the Secretary-General of the United Nations.

Article 67
Signing, ratification, acceptance, approval and accession

1. This Convention shall be open for signature by all States from 9 to 11 December 2003 in Merida, Mexico, and after that event at United Nations Headquarters in New York until 9 December 2005.

2. The present Convention shall also be open to regional economic integration organizations which have, least one of its Member States as Parties to this Convention in accordance with paragraph 1 of this Article.

3. This Convention shall be subject to ratification, acceptance or approval. Instruments of ratification, acceptance or approval shall be deposited with

the Secretary-General of the United Nations. Regional economic integration organizations may deposit their instruments of ratification, acceptance or approval if at least one of their Member States has done so. In such instrument of ratification, acceptance or approval, such organizations shall declare the extent of their competence with respect to the matters governed by the present Convention. The said organizations shall also notify the Depositary of any changes relevant to the scope of their competence.

4. This Convention shall be open for accession by all States or regional economic integration organizations which have at least one Member State which is a Party to this Convention. Instruments of accession shall be deposited with the Secretary-General of the United Nations. At the time of accession, regional economic integration organizations shall declare the extent of their competence with respect to the matters governed by this Convention. The said organizations shall also inform the Depositary of any changes relevant to the scope of their competence.

Article 68
Entry into force

1. This Convention shall enter into force on the ninetieth day after the inclusion of the thirtieth instrument of ratification, acceptance, approval or accession. For the purposes of this paragraph, instruments deposited by a regional economic integration organization shall not be considered additional to those deposited by its Member States.

2. For each State or regional economic integration organization which ratifies, accepts or approves this Convention shall enter into force after the thirtieth day after the deposit of the instrument of ratification, acceptance, approval or accession, this Convention shall enter into force after the thirtieth day after that State or organization has deposited the relevant instrument or at the time of its entry into force in accordance with paragraph 1 of this Article, whichever is the later.

Article 69 Amendment

1. After five (5) years have elapsed since the entry into force of this Convention, States Parties may propose amendments and transmit them

to the Secretary-General of the United Nations, who shall thereupon communicate any proposed amendment to the States Parties and to the The Conference of the States Parties to the present Convention to consider and adopt a decision thereon. The Conference of States Parties shall make every effort to reach a consensus on each amendment. If all possibilities for consensus are exhausted and no agreement has been reached, the adoption of the amendment shall ultimately require a two-thirds majority of the States Parties present and voting at the meeting of the Conference of the Parties. States Parties.

2. Regional economic integration organizations, in matters within their competence, shall exercise their right to vote in accordance with this Article with a number of votes equal to the number of their Member States that are Parties to this Convention. Such organizations shall not exercise their voting rights if their Member States exercise their powers and vice versa.

3. Any amendment adopted in accordance with paragraph 1 of this Article shall be subject to ratification, acceptance or approval by the States Parties.

4. Any amendment approved in accordance with paragraph 1 of this Article shall enter into force in respect of a Member State ninety days after the date of its deposit in the hands of the Secretary-General of the United Nations, an instrument of ratification, acceptance or approval of such amendment.

5. When an amendment enters into force, it shall be binding on those States Parties which have expressed their consent thereto. The other States Parties shall be subject to the provisions of this Convention, as well as to any other earlier issue which they have ratified, accepted or approved.

Article 70
Complaint

1. States Parties may withdraw from this Convention written notification to the Secretary-General of the United Nations. The denunciation shall take effect one year after the date on which the Secretary-General has received the notification.

2. Regional economic integration organizations shall cease to be Parties to this Convention when they have denounced all their Member States.

Article 71
Depositary and languages

1. The Secretary-General of the United Nations shall be the depositary of this Convention.

2. The original of this Convention, of which the Arabic, Chinese, English, French, Russian and Spanish texts are equally authentic, shall be deposited with the Secretary-General of the United Nations.

IN WITNESS WHEREOF, the undersigned Plenipotentiaries, duly authorized by their respective Governments, have terminated this Convention.

BIBLIOGRAPHY

AUGUSTINE, Saint. Consistency. Translation of J. Oliveira Santos, S.J, Ambrósio de Pina, S.J. São Paulo: New culture, 2000. (The thinkers).

ALBISTUR, Emilio A. La corrupción como pecado social, generadora de estructuras de pecado. Centro de investigación y acción social, Argentina, Año XLV, N. 458, p. 531-533, nov. 1996.

ALCAIN, Eduardo Morón. Cuestiones jus losó cas en La Alemania de pos- guerra: su actualidad. Buenos Aires: AbeledoPerrot, 1998.

ALCALDE, Carmen. La losofía. 1. ed. España: Bruguera, S.A., 1972. (SI NO).

Alertan por omisión en noti cación de hepatitis: Uruguay. Sin datos locales porque médicos no informan. EL país, Montevideo, Ciudades- B3, Domingo 17 de mayo de 2009.

ANDRIASOLA, Gabriel. Delitos de corrupción pública: análisis de la ley 17.060 de 23 de diciembre de 1998. Montevideo: Del foro S.R.L, 1999. (mono- grafías jurídicas 4).

ANGELL, Norman. The great illusion. Translation by Sérgio Bath. 1. ed. São Paulo: University of Brasilia, 2002. (IPRI Classics).

ARÉVALOS, Evelio Fernández. Órganos constitucionales del Estado: poder legislativo, poder ejecutivo, poder judicial, órganos constitucionales extrapoderes. Paraguay: Intercontinental, 2003.

ARGENTINA. (1853). Constitución de la República Argentina: sancionada el 1° de mayo de 1853, reformada y concordada por la convencion nacional ad hoc el 25 de septiembre de 1860 y con las reformas de las convenciones de 1866, 1898, 1957 y 1994. Disponível em:< http://www.senado.gov.ar/ web/inte- res/constitucion/preambulo.php.> Acesso em: 26.04.2011.

ARGENTINA. Codigo de etica de la funcion pública. Decreto 41/27-ene- 1999, Publicada en el Boletín O cial del 03-feb-1999. Número: 29077. Página: 5. Disponível em:< http://www.infoleg.gov.ar> Acesso em: 27.04.2011.

ARGENTINA. Codigo penal. Ley 11179/30-sep-1921, Publicada en el Bole- tín O cial del 03-nov-1921, Número: 8300 Página: 1. Disponível em:< http:// www.infoleg.gov.ar> Acesso em: 27.04.2011.

ARGENTINA. Codigo procesal penal. Ley 23984/21-ago-1991, Publicada en el Boletín O cial del 09-sep-1991. Número: 27215. Disponível em:< http:// www.infoleg.gov.ar> Acesso em: 27.04.2011.

ARGENTINA. Ley 26.388/ 4 de junio del 2008 (promulgada de hecho el 24 de junio de 2008). delitos de cuello Blanco. Disponível em: < http://www. jgm.gov. ar> Acesso em: 27.04.2011.

ARGENTINA. Ley N° 189. Codigo contencioso administrativo y tributario de la C.A.B.A. (Boletín O cial No 722- Legislatura de la Ciudad Autónoma de Buenos Aires) Disponível em:< http://boletino cial.buenosaires.gob.ar> Acesso em: 27.04.2011.

ARGENTINA. LEY No 2303/07 - Se aprueba el código procesal penal de la ciu- dad autónoma de Buenos Aires. Disponível em:< http://www. buenosaires.gov. ar> Acesso em: 27.04.2011.

ARGENTINA. LEY No 451/00 - Aprueba texto del anexo I, como régimen de faltas de la ciudad de Buenos Aires. sustituye denominación del capítulo IV del libro II, y del art. 47 del código contravencional, B.O. N° 405. EN EL anexo II deroga ordenanzas, leyes, decretos y resoluciones normas. Disponível em:< http://www.buenosaires.gov.ar> Acesso em: 27.04.2011.

ASOCIACION DE MAGISTRADOS DEL URUGUAY, abril 1998 Montevideo. El poder judicial frente a la corrupción. Montevideo: Liventa papelex S.R.L, 1998.

ARTANA, Daniel. Los costos económicos de la corrupción. Idea, Argentina, p. 91-92, ago. 1998.

Autoridades del clínicas cerraron la emergencia por falta de recursos: traslados. Los pacientes son derivados hacia otros centros. EL país, Montevideo, Nacional – A5, Domingo 17 de mayo de 2009.

BACON, Francis. Novum organum or true indications about the interpretation of nature. Translation and notes by José Aluysio Reis de Andrade. São Paulo: New culture, 2000. (The thinkers).

BAIGUN, David; RIVAS, Nicolás García (dir.). Delincuencia económica y corrupción. 1. ed. Buenos Aires: Ediar, 2006.

BAKUNIN, Michael Alexandrovich. Anarchist texts. Translation by Zilá Bernd. Selection and notes Daniel Guérin. Porto Alegre: L & PM, 2006. (L & PM Pocket Collection).

BARATTA, Principles of minimum criminal law: for a theory of human rights as the object and limit of criminal law. Translation by Francisco Bissoli Filho. published in the journal "Criminal doctrine n. 10-40. Buenos Aires: Depalma, 1987. Santa Catarina, 2003.

BARBOZA, Julio. Derecho Internacional Público. Buenos Aires: Zavalia,1999.

BARRIO, Javier Delgado; VIGO, Rodolfo L. Sobre os princípios jurídicos. Buenos Aires: Abeledo-Perrot. 1998

BERISTAIN, Antonio. Nova criminologia: a luz do direto penal e da vitimologia. Tradução de Cândido Furtado maia Neto. Brasília: universidade de Brasília, 2000.

BERLINGER, Giovanni; BOTTLE, Volnei. The human market: a bioethical study of buying and selling body parts. Translation by Isabel Regina Augusto. Brasília: University of Brasília, 1996.

Biblia. Espanhol. Santa Biblia. Versión de Casiodoro de Reina. Madrid: Socie- dad bíblica, 1995.

BRAZIL. UN. Board of control of financial activities. Money laundering: a worldwide problem. Brasília: UNDCP, 1999.

BOBBIO, Norberto. Theory of legal order. Translation by Maria Ce-east Cordeiro Leite dos Santos. 10. ed. Brasília: University of Brasília, 1999.

BRAZIL. Federal Court of Justice. Meetings of supreme courts: challenges and perspectives in the process of integration of mercosul. Brasília: Supreme Courts Forum, 2007.

CALDWELL, Taylor. An iron pillar. Translation by Luzia Machado da Costa. Rio de Janeiro: Distributor Record of press services S.A., 1965.

CARBONELL, Miguel; SALAZAR, Pedro (eds.). Garantismo: estudios sobre el pensamiento jurídico de Luigi Ferrajoli. Madrid: Trota, 2005. (colección estruc- turas y procesos serie derecho).

CASTRO, Anna Maria; DIAS, Edmundo F. Introduction to socio-logical thinking. 4. ed. Rio de Janeiro: Eldorado, 1976.

CATENACCI, Imerio Jorge. Introducción al derecho: teoría general. Argu- mentación razonamiento jurídico. 1. ed. Buenos Aires: Astrea, 2006. V. 1. Reim- presión. (Colección mayor Filosofía y derecho v. 7).

CHAUI, Marilena. What is ideology. 26. ed. São Paulo: Editora brasiliense, 1988. (First 13 steps).

CHOMSKY, Noam. Reasons for status. Translated by Vera Ribeiro. Rio de Janeiro: Record, 2008.

CHURCHILL, Winston S. Memories of the Second World War. Translated by Vera Ribeiro. 2. ed. Rio de Janeiro: New Frontier, 1995. v. 7. Printing.

CICERÓN. Los o cios. Traducción Manuel de Valbuena. Madrid: Espasa. (Grandes clásicos universales).

CINCUNEGUI, Juan Bautista; CINCUNEGUI, Juan de Dios. La corrupción y los factores de poder. 1. ed. Argentina: Fundación Argentina de planeamiento, 1996.

COLEGIO DE CONTADORES Y ECONOMISTAS DEL URUGUAY. "Cam- bios en la administración nanciera gubernamental". Montevideo: colegio de contadores y economistas del Uruguay. 1999.

COMISSIÓN DE SEGUIMENTO DEL CUMPLIMIENTO DE LA CONVEN- CIÓN INTERAMERICANA CONTRA LA CORRUPCIÓN. Colegio público de abogados de la capital federal. Buenos Aires, 2002.

COMISIÓN ECONÓMICA PARA AMÉRICA LATINA Y EL CARIBE. Balan- ce preliminar de las economías de América latia y el Carbe. Chile: Naciones unidas, 2008.

COMISIÓN ECONÓMICA PARA AMÉRICA LATINA Y EL CARIBE. Estu- dio económico de América latina y el Caribe: política macroeconómica y volatilidad. Chile: Naciones unidas, 2008.

COMTE, Auguste. Curso de loso a positiva. Traducción de Carmen Lessining. 1. ed. Buenos Aires: Need, 2004. (Ediciones libertador).

CONSEJO DE LA MAGISTRATURA PODER JUDICIAL DE LA CIUDAD DE BUENOS AIRES. La plani cación estratégica en la justicia de la ciudad de Buenos Aires. Argentina: Geudeba, 2008.

CONVENCIÓN DE NACIONES UNIDAS CONTRA LA CORRUPCIÓN: Nuevos paradigmas para la prevención y combate de la corrupción en el escenario global. 1. ed. Buenos Aires: O cina anticorrupción. Ministerio de Justicia y Derechos Humanos, 2004.

Corrupción y democracia en la argentina: La interpretación de los estudiantes uni- versitarios. Revista Argentina de sociología. Argentina, año 3, N°4, p. 9-31, 2005.

COSTA, José Armando. Legal outline of administrative improbity. Brasília: Legal Brasília, 2000.

COULANGES, Fustel de. The ancient city: studies on worship, law, institutions of Greece and Rome. Translation by Jonas Camargo Leite and Eduardo Fonseca. São Paulo: Hemus, 1975.

CRETELLA JUNIOR, José. Course of Roman law. 1. ed. Rio de Janeiro: forensic, 1968.

CHRISTIAN, Fortini. et al. (Org.). Public policies: possibilities and limits. Belo Horizonte: Forum, 2008.

CROCE, Benedetto. et al. Declarations of rights. Brasília: Rondon Project Foundation, 1988.

DARWIN, Charles. El origen de las espécies. 1. ed. Buenos Aires: centro editor de cultura, 2006.

DELMAS-MARTY, Mireille. Three of them for a world right. Translation and afterword of Fauzi Hassan Choukr. Rio de Janeiro: Lumen Juris, 2003.

DEPARTMENT OF PROTECTION AND ECONOMIC DEFENSE OF THE SECRETARY OF ECONOMIC LAW OF THE MINISTRY OF JUSTICE. Combo to cartels and leniency programs. Brasília: publication o cial, 2008. (SDE / DPDE 01/2008).

DESCARTES. Discourse of method, the passions of the soul, meditations. São Paulo: New culture, 2000. (The thinkers).

DONZELE, Patrícia F. L. Aspects of Sovereignty in International Law: Addresses the internal and external aspects of sovereignty, analyzing its subsistence in the process of integration seen at the international level. Available at: <http://www.direitonet.com.br/artigos/exibir/1496/

Aspectos-da-soberania-no-Direito-Internacional>. Accessed on: 03.06.2011.

ECO, Umberto. Como se hace una tesis: técnicas y procedimientos de investigación, estudio y escritura. Barcelona: Editora Gedisa, S.A., 1988.

EL PODER JUDICIAL ANTE LA CORRUPCIÓN. Cuaderno No 2, 2004, Montevideo. ¿Qué justicia queremos? Uruguay: asociación de funcionarios judiciales del Uruguay, 2004. 32 p.

ENGELS, Friedrich. The origin of the family, the private property and the State. Translation Ciro Mioranza. São Paulo: Scale. (Great works of universal thought - 2).

ETKIN, Jorge Ricardo. La doble moral de las organizaciones: los sistemas per- versos y La corrupción institucionalizada. España: McGRAW-HILL, 1993. p. 266.

FERMÍN, Claudio. 100 razones para salir de Chávez. Venezuela: Democracia y periodismo, 2004.

FERNANDES, A.; GAVEGLIO, S.(comp.). Globalización, integración, Mercosur y desarrollo local. 1. ed. Argentina: Homo Sapiens Ediciones, 2000.

FORO UNIÓN EUROPEA, AMÉRICA LATINA Y EL CARIBE LAS POLÍTI- CAS FISCALES EN TIEMPOS DE CRISIS: VOLATILIDAD, COHESIÓN SO- CIAL Y ECONOMÍA POLÍTICA DE LAS REFORMAS. 2009, Montevideo. El papel de la política tributaria frente a la crisis global: consecuencias y perspectivas. Montevideo: Naciones unidas, 2009. 48p.

FORO UNIÓN EUROPEA, AMÉRICA LATINA Y EL CARIBE LAS POLÍ- TICAS FISCALES EN TIEMPOS DE CRISIS: VOLATILIDAD, COHESIÓN

SOCIAL Y ECONOMÍA POLÍTICA DE LAS REFORMAS. 2009, Montevideo. Crisis, volatilidad, ciclo y política scal en América latina. Montevideo: Na- ciones unidas, 2009. 44 p.

GALES CASA CAMBIARIA LESPAN S. A. Manual de prevención de lavado de activos. Montevideo- Uruguay: Gales casa cambiaria lespan S. A., 2004. 119 p.

GALVÃO, Eduardo Rodrigues. Study of Brazilian problems. 3. ed. Brasília: Federal Senate, Graphic Center, 1985.

GILES, omas Ransom. History of education. São Paulo: EPU, 1987.
GOMÁ, Javier. Public Exemplarity. 2. Ed. Madrid: Taurus thought,2009.

GOMES, Luís Roberto. The public ministry and the control of administrative omission: the control of the State Omission in Environmental Law. 1. ed. Rio de Janeiro: University Forensics, 2003.

GRONDONA, Mariano. La corrupción. 3. ed. Argentina: Editorial planeta Argentina, 1993.

GUEDES, Je erson Cárus; SOUZA, Luciane Moessa (coord.). Advocacia de Estado: questões institucionais para a construção de um Estado de justiça: estudos em Homenagem a Diogo de Figueiredo Moreira Neto e José Antônio Dias To oli. Belo Horizonte: Fórum, 2009.

HEIDEMANN, Francisco; SALM, José Francisco (Org.). Políticas públicas e desenvolvimento: bases epistemológicas e modelos de análise. 2. ed. Brasília: universidade de Brasília, 2010.

HESPANHA, António Manuel. Cultura jurídica européia: síntese de um milê- nio. Florianópolis: Fundação Boiteux, 2005.

HOMERO. A odisséia. Tradução e adaptação Fernando C. de Araújo Gomes. São Paulo: Escala. (Mestres pensadores).

HUM AND. São Paulo: New culture, 2000. (The thinkers).

JACKSON, Philip W., et al. La vida moral en la escuela. Traducción de Glória Vitale. Buenos Aires: Amorrortu, 2003.

JIMÉNEZ, Juan Pablo; PODESTÁ, Andrea. Inversión, incentivos scales y gastos tributarios en América latina. Santiago de Chile: Naciones Unidas, 2009. (Serie macroeconomía del desarrollo).

JUNTA ASESORA EN MATERIA ECONÓMICO FINANCEIRA DEL ESTA- DO. Ética y función pública. 1. ed. Montevideo: Tarma, 2008. 60 p. (Serie: "manuales de capacitación" no 1).

JUNTA ASESORA EN MATERIA ECONÓMICO FINANCEIRA DEL ESTA- DO. Normas de conduta en la función pública. Montevideo: Tarma, 2007

KAFKA, Franz. Consideraciones acerca del pecado: cuadernos en octava. Bue- nos Aires: Ediciones libertador, 2004. (Edición especial).

KAFKA, Franz. The process. São Paulo: Martin Claret, 2000. (The masterpiece of each author).

KANT, Immanuel. Critique of pure reason. Translation by Valerio Rohden and Udo Baldur Moosburger. São Paulo: New culture, 2000. (The thinkers).

KANENGUISER, Nartín. El n de La ilusión: Argentina 2001·2011 crisis, re- construcción y declive. 1. ed. Buenos Aires: Edhasa, 2011.

KLUG, Ulrich. Lógica jurídica. Traducción de J. C Gardella. Bogotá: Temis, 2004. v. 2. Reimpresión

KNELLER, George F. Science as a human activity. Translation by Antonio José de Souza. Rio de Janeiro: Zahar, 1980.

LA LUCHA MUNDIAL CONTRA LA CORRUPCIÓN. Foro Politico: Revista del Instituto de Ciencias Politicas. v.XVI Buenos Aires: Universidad del Museo Social Argentino, Marzo 1996. p. 76-81.

LANDES, David S. Wealth and the poverty of nations: why some are so rich and others so poor. 2. ed. Translation Álvaro Cabra. Rio de Janeiro: Campus, 1998.

LENAY, Charles. La evolución: de La bactéria al hombre. Traducción y adaptación Pilar Martinez. Barcelona: RBA, 1994. (Conocer la ciencia).

LEVI, José Fernando Casañas. Legislación penal Paraguaya: código penal concordado, código procesal penal concordado, leyes complementares, acordadas y resoluciones de la corte suprema de justicia, resoluciones del ministerios público, índice alfabético. Paraguay: Intercontinental, 2006. (legislación Paraguaya edición 2006).

LOCKE, John. Essay on human understanding. Translation of Anoie Aiex. São Paulo: New culture, 2000. (The thinkers).

LOCKE, John. Second Treatise about Government. Translated by Alex Marins. São Paulo: Martin Claret, 2002. (The masterpiece of each author)

LONG, Kim. e almanac of political corruption, scandals & dirty politics. New York: Delacorte press, 2007.

MAHIQUES, Carlos Alberto (Dir.). El derecho penal: doctrina y jurisprudencia. Buenos Aires: El derecho, 2005. p. 6

MAIRAL, Héctor A., Las raíces legales de la corrupción: o de cómo el derecho público fomenta la corrupción en lugar de combatirla. 1. ed. Argentina: Ediciones Rap S.A, 2007.

MALMESBURY, Omas Hobbes. Leviathan or matter, form and power of an ecclesiastical and civil State. Translation by João Paulo Monteiro and Maria Beatriz Nizza da Silva. São Paulo: New culture, 2000. (The thinkers).

MANCUSO, Hugo R. Metodología de La investigación em ciências sociales: lineamientos teóricos y prácticos de semioepistemología. 1. ed. Buenos Aires: Paidós, 2006. 3. v. Reimpresión.

MANCUSO, Rodolfo de Camargo. Public civil action: in defense of the environment, cultural heritage and consumers. 8. ed. Brazil: Journal of the Courts, 2002

MANFRONI, Carlos A. La convención interamericana contra la corrupción. 2. Ed. Argentina: Abeledo-Perrot, 2001.

MANFRONI, Carlos A. Soborno transnacional. 1. Ed. Argentina: Abeledo- -Perrot, 1998.

Manual on monitoring of alternative penalties and measures. Brazil: pan er Graphic, 2002.

MARTINO, Antonio A. Etica y democracia. Foro Politico: Revista del Instituto de Ciencias Politicas. v.XII. Buenos Aires: Universidad del Museo Social Argen- tino, Diciembre 1994. p. 7-10.

MENDIETA, Manuel Villoria. Ética pública y corrupción: curso de ética admi- nistrativa. 1. ed. Madrid: Editorial Tecnos grupo Anaya S.A., 2000.

MENY, Yves; THOENIG, Jean-Claude. Las políticas públicas. Versión Españo- la Francisco Morata. Traducción de Salvador Del Carril. 1. ed. Barcelona: Ariel ciencia política, 1992.

MINISTERIO DE JUSTICIA Y DERECHOS HUMANOS: balance de gestion; o cina anticorrupcion. Argentina, 2000. p. 49

MINISTERIO FEDERAL DE COOPERACIÓN ECONOMICA Y DESAR- ROLLO. Carpeta de información: la cooperación alemana para el desarrollo con América latina y el Caribe. Berlim, 2005.

MONTESQUIEU. Of the spirit of the laws. v. 1. São Paulo: New culture, 2000. (The thinkers).

MONTI, Víctor Manuel. Corrupción, gobierno y democracia. Ricardo G. Her- rera (Col) 1. Ed. Santiago del Estero: UNCa, 1999.

MOREIRA NETO, Diogo de Figueredo. Four paradigms of postmodern administrative law: legitimacy, nality, and science, results. Belo Horizonte: Forum, 2008.

MORO, Tomas. *Utopia*. Traducción María Guillermina Nicolini. Buenos Aires: editorial La Página S.A. editorial Losada S.A. 2003.

NEUMANN, Ulfried. La pretensión de verdad en el derecho: y três ensayos so- bre Radbruch. Traducción Mauricio Hernández. 1. ed. Colombia: Universidad ex- ternado de Colombia, 2006. (Serie de teoria jurídica y loso a Del derecho n 38).

NIETZSCHE, Friedrich. Así habló Zaratustra. Traducción por J. C García Bor- rón. 1. ed. Buenos Aires: Centro editor de cultura, 2007.

NIETZSCHE, Friedrich. La genealogía de la moral. Traducción por Sergio Al- bano. 1. ed. Buenos Aires: Gradifco, 2007. (Pensadores universales).

NIETZSCHE, Friedrich. Más allá del bien y del mal. Traducción por Sergio Albano. 1. ed. Caseros: Gradifco, 2007. (Pensadores universales).

NINO, Carlos Santiago. Ética y derechos humanos: un ensayo de fundamentación. 2. ed. Buenos Aires: Astrea, 2007. V. 2. Reimpresión. (Colección mayor Filosofía y derecho v. 15).

NÚÑEZ, José Ariel. Manual de auditoría gubernamental: control democrático contra La corrupción y el despilfarro. Buenos Aires: Ediciones Rap,2006.

OLIVÉ, Juan Carlos Ferré. et al. Blanqueo de dinero y corrupción en el siste- ma bancario: delitos nancieros, fraude y corrupción en Europa. V. II. España: Universidad de salamanca, 2002.

OLIVEIRA, Harrison. Re exões on the misery of the northeast. Paraíba: "The union" Cia. Publisher, 1984.

OLIVEIRA, Odete Maria. Prison: a social paradox. 3. ed. Santa Catarina: Ed. Da UFSC, 2003.

OLIVEIRA, Roberto Cardoso; BAINES, Stephen G. (Org.). Nationality and ethnicity at borders. Brasília: University of Brasília, 2005. (Americas Collection).

PALACIO, Ernesto. Catilina: una revolución contra la plutocracia en Roma. Buenos Aires: Abeledo-Perrot, 1998.

THE PALOMBARA, Joseph. Politics within the nations. Brasília: university of Brasília, 1982. (Political thought 60).

PARAGUAY. Constitución (1992). Constitución de la república del Paraguay: promulgación 16 de agosto de 1992. Elaborado por Horacio Antonio pet- tit. Paraguay: Intercontinental, 2008.(tomo IV libro noveno).

PASSET, René. The neoliberal illusion. Translation by Clóvis Marques. Rio de Janeiro: Record, 2002.

PATEL, Ketan J. The master of strategy: power, purpose and principle. Translation by Ricardo Doninelli. Rio de Janeiro: Bestseller, 2007.

PEGORARO, Juan S. La corrupción como cuestión social y como cuestión penal. Delito y sociedad, Buenos Aires, Año 8, n.13, p. 6-32, 1999.

PEREIRA JUNIOR, Jessé Torres. The right to defense in the 1998 constitution: the administrative procedure and the accused in general. Rio de Janeiro: Renovar, 1991.

PORTO, Maria Stela Grossi; DWYER, Tom (Org.). Sociology and reality: social research in the 21st century. Brasília: University of Brasília, 2006

PRITZL, Rupert: Corrupción y Rentismo en América Latina. Buenos Aires: Ciedla, Fundación Honrad Adenauer, 2000.

PROGRAMA DE COOPERACIÓN CEPAL- GTZ. Memoria anual marzo 2007- marzo 2008. Santiago de Chile: Naciones unidas, 2007-2008.

PUERTO, Carlos Gonzalez del; MÓDICA, Yeny Villalba y Gisela Di (Comp.).

Compilación legislativa en materia de prevención y lucha contra la corrupción. Paraguay: Publicación del instituto de estudios en ciencias penales y sociales del Paraguay (Inecip), 2004.

QUINTA CUMBRE DE LAS AMERICAS. 5. 2009, Puerto España. La reacción de los gobiernos de las Américas frente a la crisis internacional: una presentación sintética de las medidas de política anunciadas hasta el 31 de marzo de 2009. Santiago de Chile: Naciones unidas, 2009. 57 p.

RABINOVICH – BERKMAN, Ricardo David. Derechos humanos: uma introducción a su naturaleza y a su historia. 1. ed. Buenos Aires: Quorum, 2007.

RABINOVICH – BERKMAN, Ricardo David. Principios generales del derecho latinoamericano. Buenos Aires: Astrea, 2006.

RABINOVICH – BERKMAN, Ricardo David. Un viaje por la historia del derecho. 1. ed. Buenos Aires: Quorum, 2007.

REIS, Claudio Araujo. Unity & freedom: The individual according to Jean-Jacques Rousseau. Brasília: Editora universidade de Brasília: Finatec, 2005.

CIA REPORT: how will the world be in 2010. Translation by Claudio Blanc and Marly Netto Peres. São Paulo: Ediouro, 2006.

REPUBLICA DEL PARAGUAY. Manual de procedimientos estadísticas pena- les antecedentes judiciales. Paraguay, 2007.

REPÚBLICA ORIENTAL DEL URUGUAY. Ley de fortalecimiento del sistema de prevención y control del lavado de activos y nanciación del terrorismo: ley no 17.835 del 23/09/004. Uruguay: Direccion nacional de impresiones y pu- blicaciones o ciales. 2004.

RIMONDI, Jorge Luis. Cali cación legal de los actos de corrupción en La administración pública. 1. ed. Buenos Aires: Ad- Hoc, 2005.

ROJAS, Ricardo M. Algunas consideraciones losó co-políticas en torno al problema de la corrupción. Foro Politico: Revista del Instituto de Ciencias Politicas. v. VII. Buenos Aires: Universidad del Museo Social Argentino, Abril 1993. p. 61-82.

RUGNITZ, José. La polibanda. Montevideo: La republica, 2002. (caso clave: temas de investigación de la república).

SANTOS, Jerônimo Jesus. Conduct adjustment Term. 1. ed. Rio de Janeiro: Publisher and legal bookstore of Rio de Janeiro, 2005.

SAMPAIO, Plínio Arruda. How to fight corruption. São Paulo: Paulus, 2009.

SCHIJMAN, JORGE HORACIO. La Justicia en los procesos de integración. *Conceptos - Boletín de la Universidad del Museo Social Argentino,* Argentina, Ciencias Jurídicas, p. 5, AÑO 81 – Enero – Diciembre 2006.

SCHMITT, Carl. Political theology. Translation by Elisete Antoniuk. Belo Horizonte: Del Rey, 2006.

SCHOPENHAUER, Arthur. Ensayo sobre al libre albedrío: la libertad. Traducción por Sergio Albano. Buenos Aires: Gradifco, 2006. (Pensadores universales).

SIGMUND, Freud. Obras completas. traducción por Luis Lopez. v. 2. Madrid: biblioteca nueva Madrid, 1968.

SILVA, Nelson Lehmann. The civil religion of the modern state. Brasília: esaurus, 1985.

SKINNER, Quentin. The foundations of modern political thought. Translation Renato Janine Ribeiro and Laura Texeira Motta. São Paulo: Companhia das letras, 2006. v. 4 Reimpresión.

SMITH, Adam. Vida, pensamiento y obra. España (colección grandes pensa- dores).1997.

SOUZA, Jessé (org.). Democracy today: new challenges for contemporary democratic theory. 1. ed. Brazil: University of Brasília, 2001.

SPINOZA, Baruch de. Ethics: demonstrated in the manner of geometers. São Paulo: Martin Claret, 2002. (The masterpiece of each author)

SUPIOT, Alain. Homo juridicus: ensayo sobre La función antropológica Del derecho. Traducción de Silvio Mattoni. 1. ed. Buenos Aires: Siglo veintiuno editores, 2007 (Sociología y política).

Teixeira, João Gabriel Lima (coord.). The construction of citizenship. Brasília: University of Brasilia, 1986.

TOCQUEVILLE, Alexis de. La democracia en América. Traducción de Luis R. Cuéllar. 2. Ed. México: Fondo de Cultura Económica, 1957.13.v. Reimpresión.

TODARELLO, Guillermo Ariel. Corrupción administrativa y enriquecimiento ilícito. 1. ed. Buenos Aires: Del Puerto, 2008.

TRIGUEIRO, André. Sustainable world 2: new directions for a planet in crisis. São Paulo: Globo, 2012

TRINDADE, Antônio Augusto Cançado. The exhaustion of domestic remedies in international law. 2. Ed. Brasília: publisher of Brasília, 1997.

VAINER, Ari, et al. Managing scal responsible municipal simple: annual budget law manual elaboration. Brasília: Area of communication and culture - executive marketing management, 2001.

VAINER, Ari, et al. Municipal scal accountable management: multi-year planning manual. Brasília: Area of communication and culture-executive marketing management, 2001.

VAINER, Ari, et al. Managing scal responsible municipal simple: budget directives budget manual drafting. Brasília: Area of communication and culture-executive marketing management, 2001.

VÁZQUEZ, Mariana Malet. La corrupción en la administración pública: aproximación a la ley no 17.060 normas referidas al uso indebido del poder pú- blico. Montevideo: Carlos Alvarez. 1999.

VIDAL, J. W. Bautista. From servile state to sovereign nation: solidarity civilization of the tropics. Petrópolis: Vozes, 1987.

VIGO, Rodolfo Luis. De la ley al derecho. 2. ed. México: Porrúa, 2005.

VIGO, Rodolfo Luis. La injusticia extrema nos ES derecho. 1. ed. Buenos Aires: La Ley: universidad de Buenos Aires.Faculdade de derecho, 2006. 1. v. Reimpresión

VIGO, Rodolfo Luis. Perspectivas ius losó cas contemporâneas: Ross, Hart, Bobbio, Dworkin, Villey, Alexy, Finnis. 2. ed. Buenos Aires: Abeledo-Perrot, 2006.

VIRGOLINI, Julio E.S. Crímenes excelentes: Delitos de cuello blanco, crimen organizado y corrupción. Buenos Aires: Del Puerto, 2004. (Colección tesis doc- toral 2).

VOLTAIRE. Cartas losó cas. Traducción y notas Fernando Savater. Barcelo- na: Altaya, 1993. (Grandes obras del pensamiento v. 7).

Printed in the United States
By Bookmasters